LOST ENGLISH

LOST ENGLISH

Word and Phrases That Have Vanished From Our Language

Chris Roberts

Michael O'Mara Books Limited

First published in Great Britain in 2009 by
Michael O'Mara Books Limited
9 Lion Yard
Tremadoc Road
London SW4 7NQ

A CIP catalogue record for this book is available from the British Library.

Papers used by Michael O'Mara Books Limited are natural, recyclable products
made from wood grown in sustainable forests. The manufacturing processes
conform to the environmental regulations of the country of origin.

ISBN: 978–1–84317–278–9

1 2 3 4 5 6 7 8 9 10

www.mombooks.com

Designed and typeset by David Sinden

Printed and bound in Great Britain by Clays Ltd, St Ives plc

To everyone who helped, which is
pretty much everyone – so thanks.

INTRODUCTION

English has the largest vocabulary of any language in the world. This may be because English has a magpie-like tendency to adopt words from pretty much anywhere as well as having been shaped by successive waves of invaders, bringing with them Danish, Anglo-Saxon and French words. *Lost English* reveals how some of those words have evolved and how others betray where the English themselves have invaded, or traded. The need for administrators in the far-flung corners of the British Empire meant that many Indian and Asian terms eventually made their way back home (ayah, dekko, mufti and veranda, qq.v., amongst others) and were absorbed into mainstream English. Similarly, trade links with China, the Middle East and Africa brought with them not only British prosperity, but a richer and more vibrant language, with words such as baksheesh (q.v.).

However, as new words and phrases come into the language, so others fall into disuse. Over the past thirty years there seems to have been quite a cull as Britain has reassessed its relationship with the rest of the world, and in particular the countries of the former British Empire. This, and the demilitarization of British society with the end of National Service in the 1960s, left a slew of terms adrift in the language whose use has dwindled and all but disappeared. A shame in many ways, as life must have been made richer when people referred to 'poodlefakers', 'rum coves' and 'knickerbockers'.

Many of the words and concepts in this book will be distantly familiar to the reader, who may even use them in conversation from time to time – either ironically or deliberately to invoke a rather archaic tone. However, they are no longer part of everyday language, even though they may have been common until well into the last half of the twentieth century. Some are, as mentioned above, the victims of huge socio-economic events, whilst others lost out to changing fashion, social attitudes and new technologies.

In the latter case, the words are doomed to extinction because, quite simply, the objects and practices they describe have become obsolete. Other 'lost' words occasionally make a comeback – and one of the dangers of writing a book like this is that one is setting oneself up for a fall. A hundred and fifty years ago the word 'crap' (meaning husk or waste product) would certainly have been included in a nineteenth-century version as no one in England used it any more. However, the confluence of two unrelated events that affected the lives (directly or indirectly) of everyone in Britain brought this word back in the early twentieth century.

In the early part of Queen Victoria's reign Mr Thomas Crapper perfected his flushing toilet at his workshop in Chelsea. He adopted the slogan 'a certain flush with every pull' and his lavatories sold across Britain. No one thought there was anything risible about this until the First World War, when American troops came over to the UK in their thousands. In the US the word crap was not obsolete and was used pretty much in its modern sense. Naturally the GIs thought it was hilarious, yet curiously logical, that they could take a crap in a crapper. So, in what etymologists refer to as a backwards formation, Crapper was reunited with crap in the speech of his countryfolk, and the word reappeared in Britain. Its widespread social acceptability is also an example of more recent changing attitudes to swearing. This has meant a drop-off in the use of muted oaths such as 'What the dickens!' (q.v.) and 'By Jove!' in favour of older and more robust Anglo-Saxon alternatives.

We live in an age with unparalleled access to information and easy storage and dissemination of that knowledge. We also live at a time of incredibly rapid change and this is reflected in the turnover of words as well, particularly as technologies move on and social structures shift. The latter in particular has resulted in words like 'character' (in the sense of a reference), 'beano' and 'brownie' (qq.v.) which, while never quite falling out of use, have seen their primary associations shift. Even relatively newly minted words and phrases can quickly become archaic or mutate to survive, as the examples of 'video' and 'yuppie' highlight. Despite the fact that it is hard to buy a video player and that the tapes have been replaced by DVDs (a technology unlikely to survive half the time that videos did), bands still release promotional videos, while films downloaded from the Internet are still referred to as videos. Yuppies, on the other hand, have vanished linguistically.

Yuppies were, if not exactly a new class, certainly indicative of many of the changes brought about since the

1980s in such things as financial security and, well, lifestyle (a word that has really come into its own this century). This before mentioning their key impact on the workforce and economy which has been transformed, whether one regards this as good or bad, over the past generation or so by yuppie values, and by politicians who shared those values. Politicians have, however, had a much more profound impact on spoken English in other areas, most notably with regard to what is usually referred to as incitement or inflammatory speeches. Nobody mourns the casually wounding terms used about sexual or ethnic minorities that were prevalent until quite recently, but equally the restricting of reasonable debate for fear of giving offence is an increasing worry to many sensible people, as well as to reactionary parrots in the 'yellow press' (q.v.).

It's odd that the phrase 'yellow press' (like the word 'reactionary', for that matter) has fallen from use, as we live in a golden age of exactly that. This is not the place for a discussion about the impact of mass media on contemporary culture vis-à-vis previous eras, except to say that how we speak and the words we use are changing more rapidly due to the sheer amount of (often conflicting) media sources in our lives.

They could just be hastening the evolution of language, which has been tracked back almost 30,000 years by scientists at Reading University. These researchers (using a high-powered computer known as ThamesBlue) discovered that identity words like 'I' and 'we', along with numbers and basic questions such as 'why?' are among the oldest. They also claim to be able to predict which are likely to disappear soon, including such seemingly safe ones as 'dirty', 'guts' and 'squeeze'. Apparently it is all down to which take the longest to evolve, usually numerals followed by nouns. After these come verbs and adjectives, with conjunctions and prepositions developing fastest of all.

From the speed of a word's or a phrase's evolution can be calculated its half-life; basically, the faster one arrives, the faster it leaves. This is good news if one wants to see the back of irritating modern terms; 'homer' and 'hardworking families' could die out tomorrow and it wouldn't be a moment too soon. However, it will be a shame if the deeply useful 'telly-clapping' doesn't get a decent innings:

> **Telly clapping:** Phenomenon whereby television viewers of a live sporting or other event applaud, shout and even chant as if their behaviour could possibly have any impact on the contests shown great distances away, when actually they are effectively applauding the medium through which it appears. Most often used dismissively about football fans of the SKY Four Clubs, who very often have never been to a live match and get their songs from the Internet and opinions from radio phone-in shows.

The point is that words come and go, and this book celebrates some of the most popular to have vanished – or at least to have fallen out of common usage – over the past couple of decades. They reflect, too, a lost Britain of different customs, leisure pursuits, modes of communication, curious slang and idioms, as well as the day-to-day experiences of ordinary people. In some ways this was a less strident, more innocent age, which I hope this book will allow the reader to visit.

Who now goes out to a milk bar, or can buy a penny chew? How confused might you be if someone said 'Charlie's dead' to you? If you found yourself beside a rum cove would you care? What would you do if approached by a Nippy? Could you order char and a wad in a Corner House, and if so, would a tanner cover the bill? If someone suggested the flicks, would you first take a dekko at the posters advertising the show? And would you think to order a gin and It afterwards, or take precautions with a rubber Johnny?

All these and more are to be found in *Lost English*, which gives you an opportunity to visit a vanished world that seemed to disappear while we switched the wireless from the Home and Overseas Services to digital.

CHRIS ROBERTS
London, July 2009

ADC (aide-de-camp)

Even those with the most rudimentary grasp of French might
guess that this is someone who helps in the running of a camp.
An ADC is a sort of personal assistant who ensures that things
run smoothly on behalf of a person of high rank. Originally a
military term but the usage broadened out to any sort of leading
personal aide, though in some places it is little more than an
honorary title with the holder's chief duties being ceremonial.
The role is that of an all-purpose fixer operating, in some
circumstances, alongside and sometimes over other command
structures, whose loyalty is to the individual in charge rather
than the organization as a whole. This can set up tensions and
often in literature the ADC is a slightly sleazy character used to
spy on other employees. With the post-war demilitarization of
society and ending of National Service the word has retreated
to the military and diplomatic circles it originated from. Not
that it was an entirely cushy job, as Captain Hugh Sayers, ADC
to the Governor of Bermuda, discovered in 1973 when he was
murdered alongside his boss, Sir Richard Sharples, and the
latter's Great Dane, Horsa. The killers were hanged, provoking
two days of rioting on the island.

Aggro

During what has been described as the 'golden age of soccer
violence' the chant 'A-G, A-G-R, A-G-R-O, AGRO!' (*sic*)
would be the prelude to fighting, while (depending on the

area) the refrain of 'Geordie aggro! Geordie aggro! Hello! Hello!' might act as a commentary once it had started. The word is a corruption of 'aggravation' and used to describe violent activities mainly, though not exclusively, associated with football grounds. The word, like its lumpen-shod, crop-headed practitioners ('boot boys' or 'bovver boys'), disappeared in the early 1980s as the old guard were replaced by the smart casuals, who preferred to speak of 'the business', 'tearing up', 'coming on top' or 'going toe-to-toe' when referring to their violent activities. Nevertheless, the word still survives on walls in run-down areas where councils clearly have limited budgets for graffiti removal.

Antimacassar

A cloth to keep hair oil off the covers on the backs of chairs, sofas or anywhere else a head might be lain. Antimacassars can still be seen in passenger aircraft and on trains, though rarely called by their proper name, and were first widely introduced in theatres in 1865. The word derives from Macassar oil, used as a hair dressing, and originally made with ingredients exported from Makassar (now Ujang Padang), the chief port of the island of Sulawesi in Indonesia. This popular hair treatment emerged in the early nineteenth century, though the means to combat its effects (the antimacassar) did not appear until 1850. The hair dressing was invented by a Mr Rowland of Hatton Garden – the famous diamond-trading district near Holborn in

London – and is described by the *Oxford English Dictionary* as an unguent for the hair. It even made its way into literature as an interesting rhyme in Byron's *Don Juan*:

> In Virtues nothing earthly could surpass her
> Save thine 'incomparable Oil', Macassar!

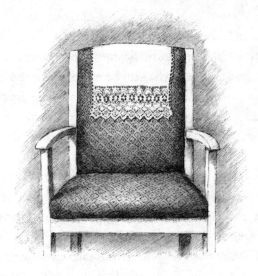

Arriviste

Like the similar parvenu (also French; literally, latecomer) this refers to a person who gains a position of power and influence without having 'paid their dues', and is consequently seen as not quite up to the job or, at best, unproven. It has fallen out of use in a social climate where mobility within the class structure is regarded as a virtue and something positive, rather than viewed with suspicion (often tinged with contempt). The arriviste would once have been seen as something of a bounder but today, given a general veneration of the new coupled with a love of change, the word has ceased to have a useful role.

Aunt Sally

Originally a game similar to skittles, in which sticks or balls were thrown at a figure, the aim being to knock it over or, in Aunt Sally's case, to knock the clay pipe from her mouth. In its meaning of something set up to be knocked over, the phrase gave rise to another definition for Aunt Sally, coming to signify anything that had been erected only to be easily overcome, and so by extension anything that is a target for criticism. Usually this meant an argument or obstacle, and the term could be used synonymously with 'straw men', which are created only to be destroyed in a debate. Sally was once to be found at fairgrounds across the country with her clay pipe and crudely painted features, but she has declined along with other traditional entertainments, notably the Southern TV series *Worzel Gummidge* (1979–81) featuring Una Stubbs and Jon Pertwee.

Ayah

This word, from Portuguese via Hindi, along with the Chinese variant 'amah' (nursemaid; also Portuguese in origin), has entered not only English but also French and German, besides Portuguese, and the meaning is the same in each case. It refers to a girl or woman employed to work in a range of domestic roles within a household, including looking after children. The word entered mainstream English through families returning from service in the Empire, along with many others including 'memsahib', who would often be the ayah's line manager, to use the modern term. Memsahib is a handy Indian construction linking the words for someone of high rank with that for a married woman ('mem' being an Indian pronunciation of 'ma'am'); 'sahib' (from Urdu, via Persian and Arabic) was a term of respect for a male, especially a Westerner, in India, and memsahib its female equivalent. Oddly enough only the female variant crossed over significantly, but both ayah and memsahib are rarely heard in Britain today, although memsahib is sometimes used jocularly or ironically, in the way that a man might refer to his spouse as 'the wife'.

Badinage

Has been all but replaced by the word 'banter' to refer to playful repartee. The term derives from the *badinerie*, a brief and lively dance which itself comes from the French *badiner*, to joke (originally from *badin*, a fool), perhaps because during such a dance humorous or witty conversation about art and life might take place. The term arose during the eighteenth century when composers, and famously J. S. Bach, began to incorporate the badinerie as a movement in the orchestral suite.

Bagatelle

Although a couple of meanings for this word (a light piece of music for piano, and a table game) are still used, albeit rarely, as a term to mean something of little value or significance it has has all but disappeared. The word has travelled from France but is based on the Italian word *bagata* meaning a trifle, something decorative but of little significance. A bagatelle might refer to a nominal amount or insignificant sum, though it might also indicate a winner nonetheless. As the slippery hero of Christopher Isherwood's *Mr Norris Changes Trains* said after a victory in court, although the sum awarded was 'a mere bagatelle, honour was satisfied'. The game, from which modern pinball ultimately derives, is named after the small eighteenth-century Château de Bagatelle in the Bois de Boulogne, Paris, where it was invented as a diversion to pass the time.

Baker day

It would be lovely to be able to say that this was a day on which children were let off school in order to spend time improving their home-economics skills; however, the real derivation is much more prosaic. The term refers to the Conservative politician Kenneth Baker (now Lord Baker of Dorking) who, as Education Secretary from 1986 to 1989, introduced the idea of national training days for teachers during school terms, which meant that pupils got a 'Baker day' away from school to lark in the parks, or whatever. The current equivalent is known as INSET (In-Service Education and Training), and both had or have the aim of allowing teachers to upgrade their skills during term time.

Baksheesh

Originally a Persian term, used in the Middle East, India and the Far East to describe a tip, a charitable donation, or a bribe. Those soliciting alms might shout 'Baksheesh!' to passersby. It entered English, along with many other terms (ayah and dekko, qq.v), through the eastern Empire and among those who lived and worked in the Colonies. The English meaning is something akin to tipping, or any money given away for a service as a show of appreciation, respect, or gratitude. It is still used in its countries of origin, though in Britain, where it was also occasionally used to mean 'free of charge', it has gone the way of beanos and besoms (qq.v.).

Ban the Bomb

This slogan belongs to a kinder, gentler age of political demonstration, when chaps wore duffel coats and marched peacefully on Aldermaston (in Berkshire, site of the government's Atomic Weapons Establishment) in company with pretty, earnest gals. Although the peace symbol, and indeed the Campaign for Nuclear Disarmament (CND) itself, have gone through various revivals since the 1960s, the simple message of banning nuclear weapons (the 'Bomb' of the slogan referring originally to the atom bomb or A-bomb and its successor hydrogen or H-bomb) has fallen victim to its own naivety. The sad thing is that today there are simply too many bombs, of too many different types, to ban, yet ironically the key stockpiles (held by the USA and Russia, formerly the Soviet Union) that CND marched against, as well as opposing the British bomb, are the only ones being reduced.

Although there are probably more pressure groups in existence than ever, the idea of a giant single-issue movement does not fit the modern world, because we no longer seem to be offered the option of one solution to fix one problem. Even the relatively simple protest against the ban on fox-hunting became consolidated in the broader Countryside Alliance (formed by the amalgamation of three existing groups), while the massive stop-the-war-in-Iraq marches of this century were actually riven by conflicting interest groups within the organizing committee.

Those three, which are far and away the campaigns that have brought the largest number of people on to the streets of London and elsewhere, all failed in their objectives. Indirectly, this failure of the mass demonstration led to the more entertaining and imaginative (and so more fashionable and media-friendly) – and sometimes illegal – protest actions of today. This is quite ironic on a number of levels, given a society in which twelve abseiling protesters dressed as foxes get more airtime and more print coverage, and influence more people, than twelve hundred thousand marching for the right to hunt the creatures.

Bassinet (sometimes bassinette)

Found in hospitals and the home, though the term carry-cot is more often used today (albeit incorrectly, as technically they are different things). The unique feature of the bassinet, which is a bed for newly born infants (originally a kind of wickerwork cradle, the word being a diminutive of French *bassin*, basin), is that it provides a warm and secure environment for very young children. They are designed to be portable, even the heavier cradle-style ones, so the child can be kept near the parent throughout the house.

Bathing dress

Quite literally what it sounds like, a dress for bathing (in the sense of swimming, rather than of having a bath) in, which, like the bathing costume, has been gradually whittled away to trunks for a man and a one-piece swimsuit or a bikini for a woman. Woollen all-in-ones for a chap have long disappeared, as have the elaborate ladies' bathing dresses often made of cotton with a trouser part beneath a skirt reaching to the knee and the upper dress part buttoned up high and covering the arms to the elbow. Although in the past the design of this heavy covering was driven mostly by a desire for modesty so as not to overexcite the chaps, modern concerns about skin cancer and over-exposure to the elements have resulted in a move back towards more flesh being hidden. Victorian concern for female modesty also brought about the bathing machine, a wheeled hut that was towed into the sea so that well-covered ladies could descend into the water virtually unobserved.

Beano

Whether the popularity of the children's comic, which took its name from this word for celebratory party with plenty to eat and drink, has consigned the word in its original meaning to the language bin of history is debatable, but certainly the meaning now most associated with it conjures up images of Dennis the Menace, the Bash Street Kids and Minnie the Minx. Nobody nowadays holds or goes to a beano, or indeed a bunfight, its slightly more genteel relation, preferring instead party, celebration and thrash, or even bash, soirée and knees-up. Similarly old-fashioned words like 'jamboree' and 'jolly' are still just about hanging on, while 'rave' has managed to reinvent itself nicely for the chemical generation. The 'beanfeast' of which beano is a jocular diminutive originated in the nineteenth century as an annual dinner given for workers by employers, beans and bacon being a prominent, if not essential, feature.

Besom

To fall into disuse in one area of meaning is unfortunate; for it to happen in two looks like carelessness. Yet this is what has happened to besom.

The first, and best-known, use is to describe a sort of broom, apparently favoured by witches, made up of a bunch of twigs bound together at one end and attached to a stout handle. They are still available, but are rarely called by their proper name, and brushes (which are pushed) are generally more popular than brooms (which sweep) as a means of dust clearance. Another product in the dust-removal department that is seldom seen is the Ewbank (or Hoky in the USA). Better known as a carpet-sweeper, this is a wheeled box inside which, when the device is pushed backwards and forwards over a carpet by means of its long handle, brushes and rollers sweep dirt into a compartment at the back, rather like a lawnmower. Although still widely available, the carpet-sweeper lacks the suction power or effectiveness of the vacuum cleaner that has all but replaced it.

The second lost use of besom is altogether different, although it may possibly have connections with the idea of 'jumping the broomstick' in lieu of an official wedding ceremony. In France, 'to burn the besom' meant to have a licentious lifestyle, and in Britain 'to hang out the besom' was a euphemism for having an affair while one's wife is away. According to *Brewer's Dictionary of Phrase and Fable* besom was once even a term for street walker (another old-fashioned and declining term). From these came, perhaps, the (now lost) phrase 'to have plenty of besom', which basically meant to have a great zest for life or plenty of spunk.

Best bib and tucker

Like 'Sunday best', this rather lovely phrase describes one's smartest (usually most formal) outfits. The bib referred to is a frill at the front of a shirt and the tucker an ornamental lace covering, both serving to protect the clothing underneath, though not quite so effectively as the modern child's bib does.

Birkenhead drill

Named after HMS *Birkenhead*, one of the first iron-hulled
ships built for the Royal Navy. In 1852, while carrying
troops and their families to South Africa, she was wrecked
near Cape Town. As there were insufficient lifeboats on
board for all the passengers the women and children were
helped into them first, while the soldiers and marines
formed up on deck in perfect military order, standing firm
until the ship foundered. This incident is widely believed to
be the origin of the phrase 'Women and children first', and
certainly established the code by which mariners, soldiers
and men in general were supposed to behave in a shipwreck,
or indeed any other disastrous situation. Most of the
soldiers and sailors on board the *Birkenhead* were drowned or
eaten by sharks, but all the women and children were rescued.
Kipling's poem celebrating the Royal Marines (nicknamed
'Jollies'), 'Soldier and Sailor Too' (1896), refers to the
incident as a drill:

> To take your chance in the thick of a rush, with
>   firing all about,
> Is nothing so bad when you've cover to 'and, an'
>   leave an' likin' to shout;
> But to stand an' be still to the Birken'ead drill is a
>   damn tough bullet to chew,
> An' they done it, the Jollies – 'Er Majesty's Jollies
>   – soldier an' sailor too!

Black and Tans

The unofficial name for the Royal Irish Constabulary (RIC) Reserve Force, one of two paramilitary forces deployed by the British government (the other being the RIC Auxiliary Division, or 'Auxies', of equally evil memory) to suppress Home Rule activists and the IRA in Ireland in 1921 and 1922, during the Irish War of Independence (or Anglo-Irish War), 1919–21. Attracted by good pay and other perks, many tough demobbed army veterans, mainly survivors of the trench warfare of the First World War, volunteered to join after the government advertised for men willing to 'face a rough and dangerous task'. They were initially kitted out in an odd mixture of service dress (khaki, hence 'tan') and RIC uniform (dark green, passing for black at a distance; occasionally the dark navy of the British police). They became notorious in Ireland for their brutalities, including the murder of a priest in Galway; it is said they earned the nickname 'Black and Tans' (often shortened to just 'Tans') in reference to a particularly savage pack of Limerick foxhounds, the Scarteen Black and Tans. (For years, and even today, the word 'Tan' was used by Irish people as a disparaging term for the English.) Their viciousness, arrogance and indiscipline were demonstrated by their sacking of Cork in December 1920, in which much of the city's centre was destroyed by fire; afterwards, some of those responsible wore burnt wine corks in their caps. Their nickname is not to be confused with the drink known as 'black and tan', which is made from a blend of ale, or occasionally lager, and stout. This has, like 'mild over stout' or 'bitter over lager' (known in some parts as 'Chinese'), pretty much disappeared from modern pubs.

Black cap

Black caps are still part of a judge's wardrobe, and are carried into the High Court and worn when the new Lord Mayor of (the City of) London is presented to the Law Courts. Their significance – and certainly widespread use of the phrase – evaporated after the death penalty was abolished for murder in 1969. In English law, the black cap was worn by a judge when passing a sentence of death, which in practice stopped in 1964. The hanging of Ruth Ellis at Holloway Prison in 1955 – the last woman to be executed in this country – strengthened public support for abolition of capital punishment. Technically, however, treason still carried the maximum sentence until 1998. This gave rise to all manner of colourful urban legends allegedly dating from unrepealed treachery acts going back to the Middle Ages and the various wars against the Welsh and Scots. Among these was the fanciful notion that making even a vaguely sexual or suggestive approach to the Queen or any member of the royal family constituted high treason, and hence a person could be executed for it. The best known use of the term 'black cap' today is as a name for a pub either at, or near, the site of a gibbet or in an area associated with the law.

Blimp

Colonel Blimp was a fictional character created by the New Zealand-born cartoonist (Sir) David Low (1891–1963) in the 1930s: an elderly, pompous, obese figure, he was a caricature of a certain type of reactionary person in the British Establishment. He became synonymous with military or administrative incompetence, complacency and heartfelt, unthinking patriotism, and gave rise to the words 'blimpery' or 'blimpishness'. Dating from the First World War, 'blimp'

originally meant a 'gasbag', a small airship or barrage balloon, later used for any kind of airship such as a Zeppelin. The word fitted Low's notion of the Colonel's character, especially its association with spluttering and bureaucratic blundering coupled with confused and often contradictory pronouncements. Colonel Blimp passionately divided opinion, or rather, people were passionately for or against him, according to their political position. A more sympathetic version of him is etched out in the 1943 Michael Powell and Emeric Pressburger film *The Life and Death of Colonel Blimp*, in which Blimp's essential good nature and bumbling sense of fair play are shown as part of a gentler world, lost in the harsh realities of the Second World War. This plump, choleric, walrus-moustached, towel-clad habitué of a West End Turkish bath replaced John Bull, Britannia and the Lion as the epitome of Britain. C. S. Lewis observed in *Time and Tide* in 1944 that, 'the future historian, asked to point to the most characteristic expression of the English temper in the period between the two wars will reply without hesitation, "Colonel Blimp".'

Blotting paper

This product hasn't disappeared (pads of writing paper still come with a sheet of blotting paper, for instance), just as fountain pens haven't entirely vanished; it's just that generally it has dropped from use in the same way that it's rare to see school desks with a hole for inkwells any more.

Blotting paper was once part of a whole array of materials that were required for writing, including spare nibs, bottled ink or cartridges, and even the inkwells mentioned above, depending on what sort of pen was being used. Its function was to mop up excess ink (or indeed any other liquid; among other things it is still used in chemistry) on a page of handwriting. This was particularly important in preventing smudging when the page was turned over. It might also be used to wipe a pen nib to clear away excess ink prior to writing.

Changing technology often presents problems and opportunities for fiction writers (hardly any novelists have really taken on board the mobile-phone revolution, for example), and the decline of blotting paper removes a handy plot device, for handwriting appears in reverse on blotting paper, allowing the sleuth to make out what has been written by holding the sheet of 'blotch' up to a mirror. Another use for blotting paper, originating in the 1960s and still around today, is its impregnation with LSD (the drug, rather than pounds, shillings and pence, LSD q.v.). A dose of the liquid hallucinogenic is dropped on a small piece of blotting paper, which is then swallowed.

Blue

A word that will never fall from the language either in its primary meaning as a colour or as a mood descriptor, though Blue Monday is now more famous as a pop song rather than as the Monday before Lent, which people traditionally spent getting very drunk. This is quite pleasing, because the Blue Ribbon Army of the nineteenth century was a band of teetotallers, originally founded in the United States but soon gaining a hold in Britain, to the extent that teetotallers in general were often called by the name, whether or not they were members of the movement. There are, however, several other meanings for blue, from drugs (amphetamines) to a form of underground party, which have vanished as fashions and tastes have altered since the 1960s.

Going out to a 'blue show' had a different meaning again, the word being associated with things that were a bit risqué or even indecent, so plays or revues of a certain kind, obscene language and most especially magazines and films were described as 'blue'. The origins of this, which go back at least as far as 1864, are a bit unclear, but could derive from legislation (Sumptuary Laws) in the USA regulating personal morals and behaviour that were known as 'blue laws'. Alternatively, according to *Brewer's Dictionary of Phrase and Fable*, the idea of 'blue pictures' evolved from Chinese brothels, the outsides of which were painted blue. In an amusingly ironic touch, 'blue books' can also refer to Parliamentary reports and other official publications put out in folio form with blue covers.

The use of 'blue' in the sense of obscene has become semi-redundant, with 'porn' or 'porno' replacing it in the context of film and other 'adult' material, and it is now rarely used to describe magazines devoted to sex. Fashions in names for these come and go: 'top-shelf', 'adult' or, slightly archaically, 'jazz mag' are among the rather euphemistic terms for such publications. 'Stag mag' has gone almost full circle. Originally used to describe the sort of smutty publications that might be passed around on a stag night, it became a general term for magazines offering pictures of naked women, only, in the twenty-first century, to return to its base; today, an online company has a 'Stag Mag' devoted to organizing the best lads' nights out.

Bob

This was a colloquial word for a shilling (twelve old pence, equivalent to five new pence); ten shillings, for instance, was known as 'half a nicker' or 'ten bob', and £1 10s (£1.50) was often referred to as 'thirty bob'. A nicker was a pound which, pre-decimalization, contained twenty shillings. The popularity of the ten-bob note (superseded by the fifty-pence coin) gave rise to the phrase 'as bent as a nine-bob note' (a denomination that never existed) to describe anything thought to be counterfeit, dodgy or abnormal. On the other hand, the going rate for Boy Scouts (now known just as Scouts) was the extremely honest bob for a job. If they were lucky they might get a two-bob bit or florin (two shillings; ten pence in today's money). Five shillings was a crown, and therefore two shillings and sixpence, or 'two bob and a tanner', was, quite logically, half a crown. With hindsight these terms for money seem much more affectionate than the way it is referred to today, for few modern coins or denominations (rhyming or market slang aside) have pet nicknames.

Bobby-soxer

This term originated in 1940s America to describe teenage girls who wore ankle-length (often white) socks with shoes, and it came over to Britain with the crooners that the bobby-soxers admired. They were less a teen tribe, like Britain's 'Teddy boys' of the 1950s, and the term was used more generally by adults to describe young girls who might attend a 'hop' (dance) or hang out at a milk bar (q.v.). It appears that the 'bobby' part has nothing to do with Bobby Darin or any other singing or matinee idol (q.v.) and instead derives from the shortness of the socks, in the same way that a bobbed haircut is short, which is also the derivation of the 'bobby pin' that accompanies such a cut. (The origin of 'bobby' in the now extinct nineteenth-century, principally Northern, noun 'bobby-dazzler', meaning someone or something remarkable or excellent, is not known.) 'Bobby-soxer' could only exist in a more innocent time, describing as it does the kind of impressionable young girl typified by Shirley Temple in the 1947 flick (q.v.) *The Bachelor and the Bobby-Soxer.*

Boche

Originally French slang, from a word for rascal, it was used derogatively to describe Germans from the nineteenth century onwards, France having felt keenly its heavy defeat in the Franco-Prussian War of 1870–1. It was picked up by British soldiers and civilians in the First World War and was in fairly common usage throughout the twentieth century. Like 'Hun', 'Jerry' and 'Fritz', but not 'kraut' (which remains depressingly popular), it fell off in the current century as a term of abuse for German people. Fritz was just a common German name, akin to calling British troops Tommy (q.v.), and Jerry a corruption of 'German', while kraut is a shortened form of sauerkraut, the chopped pickled cabbage that Germans were supposed to live on. A likely derivation of Hun, which properly refers to Central Asian peoples, is the association with the Vandals and Huns that ravaged Europe in previous centuries, much as, from the British point of view, German soldiers did in the twentieth. Kipling's poem 'For All We Have and Are', written at the outbreak of the First World War in August 1914, contains the line 'The Hun is at the gate!', a reference to the German invasion and occupation of Belgium, and which almost certainly popularized the term in Britain. In 1918 Robert Graves, who served in the First World War, published a poem entitled 'A Dead Boche', which remains one of the best-known of his war verses.

Bohemia

When estate agents start describing areas as 'bohemian' in order to increase the value of a property then there is little doubt that meaning has gone missing somewhere. Gentrification through art is now a proven regeneration tactic, but in the past to be a bohemian (thereby adopting a socially unconventional lifestyle) and live in 'bohemia' indicated poverty and low status. The link with the area of what is now the Czech Republic known as Bohemia is that in mid-nineteenth-century France *bohémien/-enne* was used to describe Gypsies, who supposedly came from that region, or who arrived in Western Europe via Bohemia, and thus the term came to be used for poor neighbourhoods. Other inhabitants of those areas (nonconformists, artists and similar) in general became known as bohemians, and so a new meaning was born.

Conan Doyle often describes Sherlock Holmes as having a bohemian nature partly because of the artistic side of his personality, but more on account of his disregard for social conventions. In the face of changing social mores (many things that distinguished the bohemians of the past, from non-marital sexual relationships to unconventional philosophical beliefs, often caused moral outrage), the word has slipped its moorings. Mention is still made of 'bobos' (bourgeois bohemians, a word for the 1990s successors to the yuppies coined by the American writer and journalist David Brooks), but at a time when alternative lifestyles are mainstream and aspirant British prime ministers embrace avant-garde artists, things have moved a long way from George du Maurier's novel *Trilby* (published in 1894), the Bloomsbury Set of the early twentieth century or even the Beat generation of the 1950s, each of which celebrated or typified bohemianism.

The simple fact is that, although the word is still used, and people even retain a grasp of its original meaning, social conditions today have conspired to render the concept, in its older sense, obsolete.

Brick
(as in 'You're a brick, Marjorie, thanks awfully!')

The word in this context belongs to another era, one of ginger ale and jolly picnics and topping japes, and a time when children were allowed adventures on their own without the prospect of litigation-happy parents or paedophile-hunting mobs appearing in their wake. The word in this sense really just means a solid, dependable, reliable and good-natured person. The phrase, perhaps oddly, was most often applied to women, yet the origin may be from King Lycurgus of Sparta (*c*.700–630 BC). When the lack of defensive walls around his city was pointed out, he simply gestured to his soldiers and said, 'There are Sparta's walls, and every man is a brick.'

Obviously this has nothing to do with 'bricking it' (to be afraid) or the conformist associations of 'another brick in the wall'. Another common use of brick is 'brick outhouse' ('as solid as a' or 'built like a', often seen as 'brick s***house'), which just means a large (usually male) person. Unless of course you follow The Commodores' 1977 song 'Brick House', which eulogized the voluptuous larger woman.

Brilliantine

A dressing for men's hair, usually a scented oil or grease (antimacassar, q.v.). This hair-grooming product (the name derives from the French *brillant* meaning 'brilliant' or 'shining') was created in the late nineteenth century by the Parisian perfumer Édouard Pinaud. Consisting of a scented and coloured oily liquid it was intended to soften men's hair and give a glossy, well-groomed appearance. It was easier to remove and not as heavy as its rivals, the lard- or oil-based pomades (or pomatums), which despite their name's derivation never smell of apples. These, like Brylcreem, though not brilliantine, have managed to survive into the twenty-first century, with its explosion of gels, mousses and other men's grooming products that permit a 'dryer' look for the hair but are not so good under a hat. In fact, the increase in newer hair-care products and styles is one of the factors in the decline of the traditional bowler-hatted City gent. Two others are the changing demographics of the City workforce in the 1980s, and, crucially, the decision by the Shell Corporation in the 1970s to stop making it compulsory for their sales staff to wear bowlers.

British warm

British Army officer's half-length, double-breasted overcoat, of thick fawn-coloured cloth with leather 'football' buttons and epaulettes, a relatively common sight until the 1970s, although originally officially adopted during the First World War. Made by the famous Crombie mill in Scotland, it was not regular issue but was widely accepted as part of an officer's 'kit', for which he would have to pay £5 15s (about £290 today) for one in 1914. The coat was intended to be worn with officers' service dress of tunic, riding breeches worn with riding boots, and peaked cap, and managed to look smart as well as being warm, practical and incredibly hardwearing. It remained an optional part of British officers' dress until long after the end of the Second World War; given the two world wars and the fact that conscription into the Army was retained until 1960, it is not surprising that the British warm continued to be a distinctive feature of men's clothing in civilian life for so many years.

Brownie

This was a simple, mass-market roll-film camera first introduced by Kodak in 1900 which, through several different models, remained popular until the 1960s. Among the best-selling of the brand were the 'box Brownie' and 'baby Brownie'. The camera (whose name, like Hoover and Google, became synonymous with the product in general) revolutionized photography by making it cheaply accessible to millions and introduced the concept of the snapshot. The very early ones were made of cardboard, and then bakelite (an early synthetic plastic), before lighter and tougher materials were introduced. In a bid to overcome many professional photographers' snobbery about the Brownie, the award-winning *Picture Post* photographer Bert Hardy (1913–95) used a Brownie camera on several assignments. Most famously, he used one to take a shot of a couple of young women sitting on railings in Blackpool in 1951 (yes, that one, with the dress blowing up), which remains among the most recognizable photographic images of any era.

Buggins's turn

Unconsidered and virtually automatic promotion, appointment or selection based on length of service rather than any qualities the favoured person might possess. This might apply equally to something relatively unimportant, such as the order of who goes in to bat during a friendly cricket match, or to positions of some influence within organizations. The earliest recorded use of the expression was by Admiral 'Jackie' Fisher (Admiral of the Fleet Lord Fisher of Kilverstone, 1841–1920), who in the early twentieth century wrote of the British Empire going down because of the culture of Buggins's turn. (The name was probably chosen to represent a typical surname.) Today, in an age that stresses meritocracy, it appears that Buggins has no place, although the Civil Service is often derided for a certain real or imagined reliance upon Buggins's turn.

Bully beef

This term comes from the French for boiled beef – *boeuf bouilli* – and has been eclipsed by the now much more common 'corned beef' ('corned' in this case meaning cured with salt); however, both refer to boiled beef compressed and tinned with a small amount of jelly. To many of the men from Britain and the Empire who fought in the First World War it would always be 'bully beef' or simply 'bully'; it also lent its name to a popular cartoon character called Bully

Beef, who, with his sidekick Chips, starred in the children's comic *The Dandy* from the 1960s to the 1990s. Expressions like 'That's bully!' or 'Bully for you!' come from the use of the word to mean excellent, and are now almost extinct. This meaning for 'bully' derives from the common noun meaning an aggressive or intimidating person, but which was originally a term of endearment for a person of either sex.

Capital!

Exclamation of delight in response to an idea or action of another, a term of high praise that conveys both approbation and congratulation. It might sometimes be preceded by another declining exclamation — 'I say!' — to emphasize the general feeling of pleasure and approval. This should not be confused with the triple version — 'I say! I say! I say!' — which was traditionally the attention-grabbing prelude to jokes told by comedians in the now equally defunct music halls.

Char and a wad

To sit down for a char and a wad simply meant to take a quick break for a sandwich and cup of tea. Heavily used among civilian staff working for the military via the NAAFI (the Navy, Army and Air Force Institutes, often irreverently known to servicemen as 'Never 'Ave Any Fags In', which supplied canteen and other facilities on British military bases), the phrase was common until the 1970s. Of the two component parts only char (for tea) has survived into the twenty-first century, though it might be amusing to ask for a wad at Prêt a Manger and see what turns up. 'Wad' presumably came about because of the wad-like nature of the bread and fillings on offer in service canteens. There is some confusion as to the origins of 'char', however, with *Brewer's Dictionary of Phrase and Fable* claiming descent from Hindi *cha*, while other sources suggest the Chinese *tcha*, from Mandarin *chá*, both words for tea. As China was the major tea producer when the drink first became popular in Britain, eclipsing coffee by the end of the eighteenth century, the latter seems more probable.

It is tempting to see the derivation of 'charlady', 'charwoman' or just plain 'char', meaning someone employed to do housework, especially cleaning, as coming from this either, in her capacity for providing tea for others, or for drinking copious amounts in the course of her cleaning. That would be miles off target, however, as would the idea of any connection with 'churl', denoting someone of low rank. Nor does the simplistic derivation from (originally) American 'chore' tell the full story. 'Char' or 'chare' actually comes from an Old English word meaning to turn, as in Charing Cross, a cross placed at a turn or bend in the river Thames. The word dropped out of use in Britain but in America, in its variant 'chore', came to mean doing a turn of work and in that form re-entered mainstream English. Having come all that way it seems a shame that chars have been replaced by having 'a lady who does' or 'a cleaner in', but the word has acquired slightly demeaning associations and has once again got lost. It is not known whether that had anything to do with the saucy Dorothy Summers playing Mrs Mopp on *The Tommy Handley Show* (Home Service and Light Programme, q.v.), whose catch phrase was 'Can I do you now, sir?'

She would very likely have sat down for a wad later, but equally she may have described her food as 'grub', 'chow', 'scran', 'snap', or 'tucker', though probably not, as a lady, 'nosebag', and certainly not 'nosh', which only arrived in 1965. It's unlikely that many of the above will be used by many people much longer except perhaps 'tucker', which the Australians think they invented but which was actually around before their continent was settled. In a Britain where food is now fashionable, with the consequence that there is a greater variety on offer than ever before, the humble wad was always doomed against the wraps, baguettes, triple-deckers or club sandwiches of today.

Charabanc

The word dates from the early nineteenth century and derives from the French *char-à-banc*, meaning a carriage with benches. Originally pulled by horses, by the twentieth century charabancs resembled elongated roofless cars or light trucks with rows of forward-facing bench seats, and were often hired for countryside outings and 'spins' to the coast. The nearest modern equivalent is probably the stretch limo, which offers the same sort of provision for groups of people to eat, drink and be mobile, though the limos seem content to cruise aimlessly around city centres. Improved public transport, coupled with wider car ownership, took the edge off the charabanc trade in the post-war period, but the term, and indeed actual charabancs, survived beyond that. The English, being English, generally pronounced the word as 'sharrabang'.

Like other archaic transport terms it is sometimes used ironically, and even found its way into pop songs by, amongst others, Van Morrison. The most attractive term for what was once a bewildering array of wheeled conveyances, phaeton, was a four-wheeled carriage named after the Greek legend of Phaeton who crashed his father's chariot (dad was Helios, the sun god) into the earth. More prosaically, hansom cabs (after their inventor, the English architect Joseph Hansom, 1803–82) were designed specifically for city use, and the term outlived the last horse-drawn taxi to work the London streets in 1946. The brougham (a light four-wheeled carriage) is never heard of today but cab (from cabriolet, a two-wheeled carriage with a hood, drawn by a single horse) and hackneys, which they replaced, are still in current use. The modern 'hackney carriage' looks nothing like its 1850s predecessor, but is still defined, according to the Taxi London website, as 'a carriage exposed for hire to the public whether standing in the public street or in a private yard.' The word 'hackney' means a harness horse with a high-stepping trot, and comes from Middle English, and originally from a French word, *haquenée*, for a docile horse or pony with an ambling gait; our use of the word may have arrived by way of the London Borough of Hackney, where horses were once pastured. Hackney coaches or cabs first appeared in London in the early 1600s, and, as vehicles plying for hire, they have been regulated by law for several centuries.

Character

Although personal references are still required by prospective employers or landlords, among others, they are no longer referred to as 'characters'. This doesn't mean that an employee's character is not important any more – rather the reverse, in fact – but that different means are used to gauge it, and broader issues considered. The other aspect of 'character' that has been lost is the notion of a general, as opposed to job-specific, recommendation, whereby the character would almost double up as a letter of introduction. This places a good deal of onus on the previous employer to tell the truth, and a broader truth than just whether a person is competent at a given task. This is particularly the case with regard to staff in serving roles that might require them to live in the same house as their employer, for it would be terrible to admit a rum cove (qq.v.) under one's roof. With this in mind the anonymous Victorian author of the *Dictionary of Daily Wants* (1858–9) devoted a section to characters, detailing the punishments for producing a false one.

> The penalties attaching to false characters are, that if any person falsely personate any master or mistress in order to give a servant a character; or if any master or mistress knowingly give in writing a false character of a servant, or account of his former service; or if any servant bring a false character or alter a certificate of character, the offender forfeits upon conviction £20, with 10s. costs.

The CV (curriculum vitae, from the Latin for 'course of life') and standard job-application letter have replaced the character as the primary documents an employer is likely to use when assessing candidates, and on these there are usually the names of a couple of senior or otherwise responsible people cited as willing to provide references, though these are rarely taken up at an initial stage.

Churching

Considering that the twenty-first century seems to be proving both more religious and more superstitious than its predecessor, it is odd that this word, which in part represents a collision of both, has vanished. In Jewish belief a woman was considered unclean after childbirth until purified (see Leviticus 12:2, for instance), whereas in the (much later) Christian faith the 'churching of women' became more a ritual celebration and blessing after giving birth. The traditional proscribed time was forty days before a woman could re-enter the church or synagogue after bearing a child, though some areas hurried the process as the time between birth and being churched was often held to be one that made a woman susceptible to attack (and even kidnap) by fairies. More practically, welfare reformers of the nineteenth and early twentieth centuries referred to the concept of churching as the time a woman should be allowed to rest and recuperate after the traumas of childbirth. In the Church of England, the Book of Common Prayer still contains a section entitled 'The Thanksgiving of Women After Child-Birth, commonly called The Churching of Women', although the practice has largely fallen into disuse in churches in the West.

Colour bar

This is a system, whether official or unofficial, under which people are denied the same rights as others on the basis of their 'race' – or, not to mince words, on the colour of their skin. Notable colour bars occurred in the post-slavery United States until at least the 1960s, and, as a legally enforced policy of racial segregation, in apartheid-era South Africa, 1948–91 (the Afrikaans word *apartheid* means 'separateness'). In the 1950s and 1960s, however, it was common to hear talk of a colour bar in Britain (although there was no such official policy); a poll in Birmingham in 1956 found that 74 per cent of respondents believed that such a thing operated in the city in employment, housing, education, and even leisure services and shops. Another poll found 98 per cent of white residents unwilling to take in coloured lodgers, often citing not their own prejudice, but that of other tenants. Similar barriers had been experienced by Irish and Jewish migrants from the nineteenth century until well into the twentieth, and these factors together led to the 1965 Race Relations Act, which outlawed any form of discrimination on grounds of race or colour. One of the many good things about the Act was that it brought about the disappearance of such overt signs of prejudice as the notices often seen in the windows of lodging houses reading 'No Dogs, No Irish, No Coloureds'.

Certain political parties attempted to make capital out of this (unofficial) operation of a colour bar among sections of the white population, notably the National Front in the 1970s, one of whose chief policies (similar to that of the British National Party today) was to reverse migration to Britain, and particularly African, Afro-Caribbean and Asian migration. This policy was once succinctly summed up by the letters KBW ('Keep Britain White'), which had become popular among such groups in the 1950s. What may well be the last surviving remnant of these once widely graffitied initials made it into the twenty-first century on St Paul's Road in Islington, North London.

The word 'coloured' to denote a person 'wholly or partly of non-white descent' (*OED*) was used in Britain until the 1960s, having originally been adopted in the 1860s by freed American slaves as a mark of racial pride. It is now regarded as offensive, except in an historical context, not least because it was an official term in South Africa for people of mixed ethnic origin.

Combination

One primary application of this word (though almost always in the plural) is to underwear, but once it would most likely have referred to a motorcycle and sidecar, in full, a 'motorcycle combination'. Also known as a 'combo' or 'outfit', for much of the twentieth century this was basically the poor man's family car, for a large-capacity motorcycle combination fitted with a double-adult sidecar could carry a family of four. They are now all but extinct on British roads, having fallen victim to the wide availability of cheap, well-made and well-equipped small cars. There is a legend (almost certainly untrue) that Herbert Austin designed the famous Austin Seven car because he so hated his foreman's BSA motorcycle-and-sidecar outfit, and determined to build a car of the same dimensions and with the same sized wheels to sell at a roughly equivalent price. For many years both the AA and the RAC motoring organizations maintained patrolmen equipped with motorcycle combinations, the sidecar being a box containing tools and spare parts. Patrolmen from the AA would salute oncoming motorists displaying an AA badge, except if there was a police speed trap in the area, the lack of a salute serving as a warning to slow down.

Confirmed bachelor

This expression is a victim of changing circumstances, for while a bachelor is still a mature unmarried man, or at least one who lives without a wife or, nowadays, a female partner, the connotations have altered. The word may come from French *bas chevalier* meaning a lowly or novice knight in the service of a more senior one ('knight bachelor' being the lowest rank of knighthood), or even a young squire in another knight's service until knighted himself, and with the addition of 'confirmed' was often used to refer to either a rampant womanizer who couldn't or wouldn't settle down, or to a man with no interest in female society. The first definition even gave rise to the expression 'gay [q.v.] bachelor', meaning an unmarried man who was out with a different female companion every night. However, the euphemistic use of 'confirmed bachelor' to describe a gay (in the modern sense) man in the period after the Second World War rather eclipsed other uses and has resulted in the term's redundancy because there is no use for the euphemism any more.

Until relatively recently, 'confirmed bachelor' was a staple of newspaper obituaries of men who never married, a useful phrase for suggesting that the subject was gay without actually coming out and saying so in hard print. Such a notice might end: 'A confirmed bachelor, he retained his interest in the Scout movement into old age.' Similar euphemisms were used by obituarists for other types, such as 'Although there were some who questioned his business methods' (for which read 'He was a thumping crook'), and 'It is true that she did not suffer fools gladly' ('She possessed a sudden, irrational, unpredictable and frequently violent temper').

Co-respondent

In the days before 'guilt-free divorce', this was a legal term applied in divorce proceedings to the person with whom a spouse (the 'respondent') had — or had allegedly, in a contested divorce — committed adultery. There was even a kind of chap (co-respondents were almost always men) who would act as a paid co-respondent to hurry along a case when adultery would speed the matter through better than other charges. These 'fancy dans' (poodlefakers, q.v.) might be seen escorting the respondent in and out of a seaside hotel (Brighton seems to have been a favourite) for the benefit of a watching private investigator, who would also have been engaged to provide evidence for the court case, often taking a photograph of the adulterous couple (sometimes, if the private eye could bribe a chambermaid for a key to the couple's room, *in flagrante delicto*). The sort of living enjoyed by the professional or habitual co-respondent, whose heyday seems to have run from the 1920s to the 1950s, could only be made by a disreputable and louche fellow wearing noisy clothes. There is an urban legend that 'co-respondent shoes' (a decadent style of two-tone brogue, either black and white or brown and white, popular in the 1920s, although the term is hardly used nowadays; they are properly called 'spectator shoes') acquired their name through association with the rather rum coves (qq.v.) that wore them, possibly because leaving such highly noticeable footwear outside an occupied hotel room, as if for cleaning, tacitly indicated that hanky-panky was taking place inside. In short, the paid co-respondent was just the sort of fast Terry-Thomas type who might well persuade another man's wife to spend time with him at a discreet hotel, probably by the sea.

Cosmopolitanism

Since the success of the magazine *Cosmopolitan* (relaunched as a women's magazine in the States in the mid-1960s; the British edition was launched in 1972) the word 'cosmopolitan', meaning at ease in, and knowledgeable about, many countries or cultures, has come to evoke a smart, clever, fashionable and well-travelled person, especially a female. As a philosophical and even a political concept, however, cosmopolitanism is the idea that all of humanity belongs to a single moral community running counter to ideologies based on patriotism and nationalism, and may, or may not, suggest support for a world government. As such it is one of a handful of words used dismissively by opposing extremes of the political process. 'Rootless cosmopolitan' was a euphemism deployed from the late 1940s by Josef Stalin to attack foreigners and 'unpatriotic' elements within Soviet Russian society, including Jews. This use was taken up by some groups in the West as well, particularly after the end of the Second World War when, in the light of the exposure of the horrors of the Nazi death camps, overt anti-Semitism became unfashionable. In consequence, right-wing politicians would often talk euphemistically of cosmopolitanism 'sapping the national identity', rather than of the supposed Jewish conspiracy that they were actually targeting.

Counterpane

A type of bedspread, usually a fairly substantial coverlet serving as the topmost covering for a bed. Laid over the blankets and sheets, it has largely been superseded by the modern duvet or 'Continental quilt'. It is an alternative to the older word 'counterpoint' meaning stitched quilt. This might often be very ornate and pictorial, allowing the imagination to fly as it did for Robert Louis Stevenson (1850–94), whose *A Child's Garden of Verses* (1885) contains a poem called 'The Land of Counterpane'. In it, he recalls lying sick in bed with all his toys close at hand, spending happy hours playing with them among the rumpled bedclothes: toy soldiers and 'ships in fleets', miniature trees and houses:

> I was the giant great and still
> That sits upon the pillow-hill,
> And sees before him, dale and plain,
> The pleasant land of counterpane.

Courting

Of all the categories of 'lost' words, the language of love is potentially the most fraught with difficulty because its vanished or half-forgotten words or phrases have a habit of coming back into use. 'Courting' is the wooing of a person to whom one is attracted, while to 'be courting' means that a relationship (with that person) has been entered into; the word carries the implication that marriage is intended, at least by one of the parties. The word's origins lie in the Middle Ages and it ties in with the highly idealized concept of courtly love and the (often hopeless and generally unconsummated) wooing of fair (and usually married) ladies by gallant knights, but the twentieth-century use conveyed a blunter (and more egalitarian) meaning, equivalent to the almost equally dated 'stepping out with', or the American idea of 'dating', which might lead to couples 'going steady'. Traditional courting contained a strong element of winning a person over, which in turn meant in some way gaining parental approval, as Michael Corleone in the film *The Godfather* (1972) discovers: 'I wanna meet your daughter, with your permission and under the supervision of your family. With all — respect.' He is somewhat hampered in this by the fact that he has to press his suit through a translator, but even within the same language the separate dialogue of desire can be very difficult. Today, some newspapers, magazines and websites rely on little else than people's interest in who is courting whom and who is going steady, though as often as not the phrases 'seen exiting a fashionable restaurant with . . .' and 'hotel romp' are used. 'Hooking up' or 'hanging out' can lead to 'necking' (spooning, q.v.), and sometimes, to use that annoying American phrase, to 'getting to first base', all of which may lead to someone becoming a 'main squeeze', 'partner' or (again in tabloidese) 'live-in lover'.

Cove

Perhaps ironically, a cove being generally a conventional, home-loving sort of body, the word may be derived from the Romany *kova*, which simply means a person or thing. In a very competitive field, cove is one of the nicest words for 'man' in the English language. In the great selection of terms where a chap is different from a fellow who is not the same as a bloke and definitely not a geezer, cove sits somewhere apart again. Often in order truly to delineate a 'cove' one has to employ a qualifier such as 'rum' (q.v.) or 'friendly', because coves on their own are just ordinary, unremarkable bodies (apart from 'interestin' coves', of course). Perhaps because of that, the word has ceased to be used in everyday English (except occasionally humorously or ironically), despite having been employed in this sense since the sixteenth century.

Darby and Joan

This phrase refers to a devoted elderly married couple who contentedly live an ordinary sort of life, often in fairly reduced circumstances. It seems to have originated in a poem called 'The Joys of Love Never Forgot' by Henry Woodfall, published in *The Gentleman's Magazine* in 1735, and has been picked up and used by other poets, novelists (including Thackeray, Trollope and Henry James), and music-hall artists, among others, until well into the twentieth century. The 1909 music-hall number 'Darby and Joan' (sung on stage by 'Joan') contains the verse:

> Darby dear we are old and grey,
> Fifty years since our wedding day.
> Shadow and sun for every one,
> As the years roll by.

The phrase is little known in the United States, although the Oscar Hammerstein/Jerome Kern song 'The Folks Who Live On The Hill', from the 1937 movie *High, Wide and Handsome*, has the line: 'Darby and Joan who used to be Jack and Jill'. When Peggy Lee came to record the song in 1957, however, the old couple had become 'Baby and Joe'.

Although there are many Darby and Joan clubs for elderly couples still in healthy existence in the UK, the phrase's decline in common usage may have something to do with a general dissatisfaction with simple contentment, rather than with the growth in disdain for the institution of marriage, or with uncertainty about the desirability of long-term relationships. The modern world does seem to militate against long-term relationships, but much more it rails against the quiet life of undemanding pleasures. As a result, we seem to be increasingly encouraged to be dissatisfied with simple pleasures, and must always seek more extreme delights and tick off lists of 'must do' things before we die. Those lists never include sitting next to the same person for decades enjoying a cup of tea, shared contentment and a nice garden.

Dear John (letter)

There is a great deal of speculation over the choice of the name John for an anonymous or as yet unnamed male, but it seems to have been adopted in the late Middle Ages as a term for a man, and for a number of professions, including those of priest and, later, a policeman. Thus we go from the American John Doe (a US legal term for an unnamed plaintiff in a case, and so, in police work, an unknown male suspect or victim, often a corpse that has yet to be identified) to John Smith (a generic term in English for a typical male citizen, akin to more modern 'Joe Bloggs') to a prostitute's client (a john, a usage that dates from the early 1900s). Since it is probably American in origin, the phrase 'Dear John' may have come from a popular American radio show of the 1930s and 1940s entitled *Dear John*, and which always began with those words, although it is more likely that 'John' was used as it is in 'John Doe' or 'John Smith' – as just a name for your ordinary average man. The term arose, probably among US servicemen, during the Second World War, which, among many other upheavals, wrought havoc on relationships, with more women working and travelling and many men away fighting. This introduced new stresses (and opportunities) that provided great challenges to many couples. The phrase alludes to the beginning of a letter sent by a woman to her husband, lover or boyfriend, detailing her desire to end the relationship. The terse opening greeting, 'Dear John', rather than an expected endearment such as 'Dearest' or 'Darling', would almost certainly have been enough to warn the recipient of the letter's contents.

Dekko

Derived from the Hindi verb *dekna* meaning to see, by way of *dekho!*, 'Look!' Dekko, or more commonly the phrase 'Let's have [or take] a dekko' was one of the linguistic gifts of the Empire. Hundreds of words bled into mainstream English from the first involvement with India in the seventeenth century. Many of these (pundit, atoll, cot, bandana and curry, for example) referred to specific objects whose meaning has stayed static, while with others (juggernaut, punch and bungalow, originally from the Hindu deity Jagannath, 'five' or 'five kinds of' in Sanskrit, and the adjective Bengali, respectively), the sense has slipped slightly. Dekko spread from the Colonial Service and into the general population via the military and has fallen from use as other words became more fashionable, and with the disappearance of the colonial and military classes that had popularized it. A similar but not quite as venerable foreign word meaning much the same thing, 'shufti' (1940s military slang, from the Arabic for 'try to see'), has managed to survive longer partly due to its use on a popular TV show, but may also be on the way out.

Dolly

An old-style, principally Victorian, wooden washing device used to stir the laundry in a tub to enable better mixing of the soap and water and to agitate the clothes. They came in two sizes – a single-handed version that looked like a sink plunger, having a metal cup drilled with holes at the end of a wooden handle about eighteen inches long, and a much larger one standing a little under three feet high. This consisted of a wooden pole or shaft fitted with a cross-piece at its upper end, with a circular base from the underside of which projected anything from three to six wooden 'legs', each about six inches long, so that the whole implement looked something like a cross attached to a small wooden stool. This type of washing dolly looked similar to something once used to torture witches, and certainly women operating the device would have found it an arduous trial. The 'stool' end was plunged into a tub of laundry and then twisted using the cross piece to beat and stir the clothes. The washtub was sometimes referred to as a dolly-tub, with zinc models replacing the earlier wooden-barrel types, and acted as a precursor to the washing machine.

There is a decent case to be made that of all the inventions of the twentieth century, the electric washing machine has saved the most people the most time. Even after indoor plumbing became pretty much universal, washing day was a chore involving heating water, and soaps, and scrubbing (or using a washing board, q.v.), and starches, and mangles to wring out and part-dry the clothes. The wringing-out, of course, came after the heavy work of using the dolly, before hanging the wash out either on a line or, often in rural areas, on hedges of sweet-smelling bushes. New and more effective soaps advertised themselves as saving time, one for Sunlight insisting that 'unless the wash has been done the Sunlight way your servant's back will be stiff and lame,' having been on her feet all day. However, the basic dolly and mangles remained pretty common until well into the last century.

The stringing together of dolly with another 'domestic' word, mop, brought about an entirely different meaning. Dolly mops were inexpensive prostitutes (doxy, q.v.) and the term, which originated in the eighteenth century, was current into the twentieth. It possibly derives from the ancient tradition of Mop Fairs or Mops. These were hiring fairs held each autumn where, according to one theory, people seeking employment would advertise themselves for sale by wearing a tassel or mop occasionally made of specific materials to signify their speciality – so, for example, a shepherd might wear a mop of wool. (Another derivation suggests that a female domestic servant looking for work at one of these fairs would carry a mop or mop head.) 'Dolly mop' originally signified a mistress, then a prostitute, but by the late nineteenth century was used to describe an amateur on the game. These were largely drawn from the serving classes, who preferred to earn their money with rather less manual labour than that required by the washing dolly.

Dolly bird

This term will never leave our lives entirely as long as there are television screens to fill at Christmas and *Carry On* films are still considered an acceptable way to fill them. Even so, non-ironic use of the phrase in everyday speech has gone. Either constituent part, 'doll' or 'bird', is still in use to mean a woman, but other terms to describe attractive, fashionable, but not overly bright, young women have replaced dolly bird. This may not be entirely due to the phrase itself being offensive, or even to changing fashion in words, but rather changing attitudes to the kind of bloke that might use a term like 'dolly bird'. It is somehow very 1970s, and reeks of cheesecloth shirts, Rod Stewart, Brut aftershave, Double Diamond ale and T-shirts featuring pigs making love under the legend 'Making bacon'. Quite simply, the expression has lost its cachet, and the bird has flown the fist.

Domestic

Like ayah (q.v.) and char (*see* char and a wad), as well as skivvy and slavey, this slightly demeaning term for a servant who performs menial chores in the home for limited pay has slipped from use. Job titles now tend to be more specific (cleaner or nanny, for example), and the traditional 'lady who does' has reinvented herself as a multi-tasking specialist within the household hygiene and allied industries, whereas a 'domestic' today just means, in police parlance, some violent aggro (q.v.) between a couple.

Donkey jacket

Simple, three-buttoned, single-breasted, unlined coat, often with a panel of PVC or other waterproof material over the upper shoulders reaching about a third of the way down the back. Made of rough, thick woollen cloth, it covered the upper half of the body down to about mid thigh. Usually dark blue or black, it was in effect the uniform of working men in heavy industry (and other sectors) at a time when Britain still had heavy industry (the name possibly deriving from the fact that it was these who did all the donkey work). Although donkey jackets could be bought in shops (and were, in large numbers), by far the largest providers were the nationalized industries like steel and coal, as well as the Post Office and the then nationalized railway. These would have a plastic fluorescent high-visibility strip across the shoulders so the wearer could be seen in conditions of poor light, and the large square pockets were useful for storing small tools. Occasionally, as with the safety tabards worn today, the company logo would be printed on the fluorescent strip (except that it wouldn't have been referred to as a logo then). They were not stylish items but nevertheless they had a certain fashion cachet, a kind of working-class chic, and it was certainly hipper to have one with a fluorescent panel of bright orange, which denoted British Steel, or of white, indicating the NCB (National Coal Board), than a shop-bought one with a standard black panel.

The decline of donkey jackets has nothing to with campaigns for the ethical treatment of animals, as no donkeys were involved in the coat's manufacture. It may, however, be connected to former leader of the British Labour Party, Michael Foot, who was widely reported as wearing a donkey jacket at the Remembrance Day wreath-laying ceremony at the Cenotaph in Whitehall in the early 1980s. There was a good deal of public tut-tutting, especially in the conservative press, at this apparent show of disrespect, but as Foot's wife pointed out, he was actually wearing an expensive short overcoat that she had chosen for him.

Doodlebug

A rather quaint nickname for the V-I 'flying bomb' (the 'V' standing for German *Vergeltungswaffe*, meaning retaliatory or revenge weapon), a primitive guided missile that was fired at London from launch sites in Nazi-occupied France towards the end of the Second World War, beginning in June 1944. The nickname 'buzz bomb' or 'doodlebug' came from the buzzing sound made by the weapons' pulse-jet engines, which could be heard from a considerable distance. In essence the forerunner of the cruise missile, the V-I had a targeting system that caused it to dive after a certain distance had been covered; however, a design fault meant that the sudden dive starved the engine of fuel, causing it to stop.

People ran for cover when the buzzing stopped, knowing that they had about fifteen seconds of terrifying silence prior to impact. Some 10,000 V-1s were fired at England, with about one in four reaching its target (chiefly London), killing over 6,000 people, with nearly 18,000 seriously injured. Barrage balloons, traditional anti-aircraft fire and even attempts by fast fighter aircraft to knock the missiles off course met with limited success, and the best approach was direct interception by fighters, whose cannon fire accounted for more than 1,000 V-1s, although by August 1944 technological developments for anti-aircraft guns had greatly increased their success rate.

Although the V-1 campaign caused considerable alarm among civilians, not everyone was scared. As comedian Paul Merton explained, his family never sheltered during the bombardment because his father had been told that the bomb with their name on it would never be made. Merton added as an afterthought that, 'Of course, it wasn't the same for Mr and Mrs Doodlebug next door.'

Doolally tap

A form of madness or cabin fever, the term originating in the early twentieth century as a corruption of Deolali, a town about eighty miles north-east of Bombay (now Mumbai). There was a large (British) Indian Army transit camp there which was the final staging post for soldiers waiting to return to Britain (the 'tap' part of the phrase comes from the Urdu word for fever or torment). Troops might wait months for the ships to take them home, and found the tedium of unstructured waiting difficult, with many getting into trouble, fighting and generally going off the rails. This condition became known as 'doolally tap', later shortened to 'doolally' as an adjective meaning anything from eccentric to temporarily insane. While the word doolally is still with us, and is applied to anyone, rather than just soldiers, the full expression vanished from everyday use in the mid-twentieth century.

Dottle

A fairly unattractive by-product of pipe smoking which thrifty smokers, including Sherlock Holmes, would sometimes recycle by leaving it to dry out before relighting it, though it was more common to dash out the dottle directly into a fireplace. (The word is from Old English *dott*, meaning, equally unattractively, the head of a boil; by the late 1500s it had come to mean a lump or clot, and so by extension dottle came to mean a plug for a container.)The decline in real fires and in pipe smoking has led to a drop off in this practice, and consequently to a decline in the use of the word at all. In essence, dottle is the soggy residue of tobacco left at the bottom of the bowl of a pipe which, if not cleared, will sour a fresh fill of tobacco. It is caused by a combination of damp tobacco and saliva from the smoker, who may increase the amount of dottle by puffing too fast.

Pipe maintenance, including cleaning (to remove a build-up of vaporized oils and other by-products) and sweetening (to clear the after effects of those), is a declining art. In fact, many of the words – and implements – associated with (tobacco) pipe smoking will probably soon be lost to most people. The rituals of smoking will always remain, however, if only through Holmes who, when confronted with a particularly intractable problem, might grade it by the number of pipes he'd have to smoke before solving it. In Ian Fleming's James Bond novels, 007's boss, the enigmatic M, displays many more of the traditional behaviours of the pipe smoker in using his pipe to disguise or reflect what he is thinking. Not least of these is the dashing of the dottle into a bin when he's made up his mind.

Doxy

An archaic term for a sexually promiscuous woman, possibly from the obsolete Dutch word *docke* meaning doll. The problem with words like this, such as 'bint' (from the Arabic for daughter), 'baggage' (beautifully used by Dylan Thomas in *Under Milk Wood* to describe Lily Smalls) or 'brass' (for prostitute or loose woman), is that they sometimes seem to have vanished, only to be picked up and become fashionable again. Film and television writers are particularly guilty of resurrecting odd old terms and putting them in the mouths of their creations to denote a quirkiness of character.

Slang terms for loose young women are numerous, and

doxy, bint and brass are not as harsh as some, while gay (q.v.) in this context has entirely disappeared. In fact, to be dismissed as a painted doxy by an elderly relative might even be seen as an indication of getting something right. In the past, though, 'painted doxies' would be advertised by madams in London's Bankside and, later, Covent Garden, alongside other 'beauties of all complexions, from the cole-black clyng-fast to the golden lock'd insatiate, from the sleepy ey'd Slug to the lewd Fricatrix.' (From *The Criers and Hawkers of London: Engravings and Drawings by Marcellus Laroon*, edited by Sean Shesgreen, 1990; Laroon's engravings date from the late seventeenth and early eighteenth centuries.)

Dry county

It is hard to believe that it is only a little over a decade since pubs and off-licences were permitted to open all day on a Sunday. This meant the end of many traditional Sunday activities including the late dash to the 'offy' before it closed, the sedate and time-controlled pre-lunch pint, the afternoon lock-in, alongside many other strange activities in which the thirsty had to indulge to get booze on a Sunday. Many parts of the country – notably Scotland, where for many years only 'bona-fide travellers' could buy a drink on a Sunday – were once 'dry' altogether on the Sabbath, and parts of Wales held firmly to this tradition even beyond the 1995 liberalization of the licensing laws. This led to quite odd social phenomena, such as Conservative and Unionist Clubs having often huge memberships in predominantly Labour-voting mining areas. The explanation lay in the fact that private membership clubs (and hotel bars) could avoid the Sunday ban on alcohol sales, as could local railways, leading in some places to a surge in use of certain routes on Sundays.

Egg on your chin

A polite way of telling a man that his fly zipper or buttons are undone (although women often wear trousers, the expression does not seem to be directed to them). The phrase is one of a number of similar euphemisms, another being 'stars in the east', which were used, somewhat genteelly, to draw attention to the problem without mentioning it directly, and probably came about as a way of alerting a man when in mixed company, thus avoiding embarrassing the women present. The female equivalent, to warn that a petticoat is showing below the hemline, is 'Charlie's dead' (appropriately, the name of a restaurant that opened fairly recently in Petticoat Lane, London). It is easy to see why this one fell from favour, because as fashions change showing one's petticoat (which are no longer widely worn) might be a deliberate statement. The derivation of 'egg on your chin' could be that the gentle hint might avoid a person getting egg on their face (serious embarrassment) if they carried on unchecked. There is, however, no connection between 'Charlie's dead' and 'Queen Anne's dead', which is an archaic way of saying that someone is very late with their news (the monarch in question having died in 1714).

Eiderdown

This refers either to the 'down' – the soft, fine insulating feathers – of the eider duck, or to a form of bed quilt filled with that down. Essentially, an eiderdown acts as a kind of over-blanket laid on top of the other bedclothes, typically sheets and (in pre-central heating days) a number of blankets; should the bed's occupant become too warm, it is easy to throw the eiderdown off, as, unlike blankets and sheets, it is not tucked in. The eiderdown seems to have been completely usurped by the duvet, or in America by the slightly odd-sounding 'comforter'. Duvets (or 'Continental quilts', although they are not quilted) come in different ratings indicating how warm they are, and a range of sizes to complement beds of different dimensions, from single via twin and queen up to king, and can be filled with cotton, silk, or synthetic fabrics, and, rarely, feathers. The triumph of the duvet over the (often heavier) eiderdown is probably because of better heating in houses, more people with allergies and a general move away from the heavier fabrics and clothing of previous eras; it is also much easier to make a bed by simply straightening the sheets and the duvet, than to rearrange sheets, blankets, eiderdown and, perhaps, counterpane (q.v.).

(In one of those curiosities of words borrowed by English from other languages, French *duvet* means down – as in feathers – and what is called a duvet in English is generally called *une coquette* in France, although *le duvet* now seems to be catching on there.)

Fancy goods

It would be pleasing to think that these are so called because one only buys them if one fancies them, but realistically the derivation is from the ornate (or fancy) nature of the items, which have a primarily ornamental use. (The expression seems to have originated in the early nineteenth century – New York's famous jewellery store, Tiffany & Co., was founded in 1837 as a 'stationery and fancy goods emporium' – while 'fancy' in this meaning dates from medieval times, as a contraction of 'fantasy'.) There is a definite overlap with gimcrack (q.v.) products, and though the term 'fancy goods' is still used in the wholesale trade, members of the public tend nowadays to refer to 'gift items', or even 'souvenirs' or 'impulse purchases'. Department stores no longer have fancy-goods sections, because today such items are so widespread across different areas of the store, nor, sadly, did one feature in Grace's Department Store, the setting of the popular television sitcom *Are You Being Served?*, which ran from 1972 to 1985. Even so, one can still sometimes find old-fashioned shop fronts including the phrase 'Fancy Goods' (usually with 'Stationery' as well) in the list of wares on offer inside.

Flicks (US: flickers)

First used in the 1920s to describe films or as a generic word for the cinema (as in 'Let's got to the flicks'), the word was still quite widely used in the 1970s. Its most likely origin is the obvious one: the erratic nature of many early projections, which offered a rather different experience from today's high-definition movies. The flickering was caused by the rate of frames per second (fps) as the film passed through the projector. A projection speed of 40 fps reduced the flickering but led to other issues with the available technology (which can best be put under the heading 'health and safety', as this was chiefly overheating of the projector, which sometimes caught fire), so often the projections had to run at a lower rate. Advances in film technology rendered the phenomenon obsolete long before the term fell out of use.

This is possibly because although the projectors had improved, as had film, colour and sound, British cinemas themselves had often remained more or less the same, so offering a clear link back to the age of the flicks. The cinema renaissance since the 1980s (when it was feared video would wipe out film-going) has led to the closing of many of the old 'fleapits', with their single screens and ageing, musty seats, and the opening of multi-screened modern venues. This initially brought about a reduction in the number of cinemas. Brixton in South London once had as many as eight, for example, but now has one, despite a gradual increase in the number of cinemagoers since the trough of the early 1980s. In 1984 10 per cent of under-fourteens went to the cinema once a month, 16 per cent of fourteen-to-twenty-four-year olds, 4 per cent of twenty-five to thirty-four-year-olds, and only 1 per cent of those over thirty-five. By 2000 these figures were 32, 54, 3 and 14 per cent, respectively. In overall numbers these figures are still down on the peak years, with 167 million cinema visits in Britain in 2003, compared to 1,400 million a year in the 1940s, when audiences packed the flicks to see double features, B movies, weepies and westerns.

Four-eyes

A very simple-to-use insult for anyone with glasses, the word 'speccy' added before it completing the abuse. Other derogatory terms like 'Joe 90', 'Magoo', 'Deirdre' or 'Ant and

Decs' (rhyming slang for 'specs') rely on characters transiently in the public eye (if you'll forgive the pun). In the modern world of contact lenses and laser eye surgery, however, wearing glasses has become increasingly a lifestyle choice. Pop stars in the 1980s started the trend for 'cosmetic' disability aids and since then there has been 'librarian chic', 'geek chic' and, more distressingly, a subsection of pornography devoted tospectacle-wearers. All of which rather gives the lie to the famous line by Dorothy Parker that 'Men seldom make passes / At girls who wear glasses.' Additionally, according to Dr Erin Heerey of the School of Psychology at Bangor University in Wales, teasing and, even unpleasant, nicknames are an 'essential part of life' and are actually positive for children's development, helping rather than hindering their social skills. In fact, though, 'four-eyes' has largely fallen out of use, as has the older and even more archaic 'gig-lamps', a term for glasses, or a name for someone who wears them, originating from the oil lamps on a gig, a light two-wheeled carriage drawn by a single horse.

Galloping consumption

'Consumption' was once the most commonly used term for tuberculosis (TB), and is a vividly horrible way of describing how the disease consumes and wastes its victims. (An even older word for the disease, phthisis, comes from Classical Greek *phthinein*, meaning 'to decay'.) It is a common, highly infectious and often deadly bacterial disease that has been with us since ancient times, killing hundreds of millions of people over scores of centuries. The more severe form (miliary TB) is known as 'galloping consumption' on account of the speed of its spread and effects. Hopes that the disease might be eradicated altogether, at least in developed countries and largely through vaccination programmes, were dashed when antibiotic-resistant strains of the disease began to appear in the 1980s, something exacerbated by widespread immigration of people, often refugees, carrying the disease. Although modern drugs combat TB far more effectively than the old fresh-air sanatorium cure, the illness is still widespread, and its effects are typically worst among the poorest people. (The idea behind sanatoriums, of segregating patients, has rather disappeared for serious illnesses like TB, but all sorts of health clinics still exist for detoxing patients, or for rest cures of various types.) Despite its horrors, consumption has always had a sort of 'deathly chic', not merely because so many writers, poets, composers, singers and actresses fell victim to it, but also because it was a recurring theme in novels and operas, from Alexandre Dumas *fils*'s 1848 novel *La Dame aux camélias* (on which Giuseppe Verdi based his opera *La Traviata*, first performed – disastrously – in 1853) to Thomas Mann's novel *The Magic Mountain* (1924), which is set in a TB sanatorium. Away from fiction, at least two and probably all three of the Brontë sisters who survived into adulthood died of consumption, as did their brother, Branwell. Other famous victims of the disease include the poet John Keats and the American dentist and gunfighter John Henry 'Doc' Holliday, whom his friend Wyatt Earp described as: 'A long lean ash-blond fellow nearly dead with consumption, and at the same time the most skilful gambler and the nerviest, speediest, deadliest man with a gun that I ever knew.'

Galoshes

A galosh (though the plural is more usually seen) is a kind of waterproof overshoe, usually made of rubber, worn over other footwear to protect it, although the term was sometimes also used for any protective waterproof boots.

The word (which appeared in the mid-nineteenth century and derives originally, via a Middle English word for a clog, from Latin gallica, meaning a 'Gallic shoe') has been replaced in popular use by 'overshoes', or sometimes by 'wellingtons', though strictly speaking the latter are not the same thing, since 'galoshes' refers to any form of protective overshoe, and originally were not necessarily made of rubber. Either way, outside of the shoe trade and the fetishist market the term is in danger of disappearing, although galoshes are still readily available, albeit generally under the term 'overshoes'; they are rarely seen in this country nowadays, however. The word has also vanished from the product catalogue of the Finnish company Nokia, which was a major producer of galoshes and rubber boots in its pre-mobile-phone days.

Gasper

This dated slang word for a cigarette (especially a cheap one) is used to good effect in Sarah Waters's 2006 novel *The Night Watch*, set in and just after Second World War, in which the heroines regularly light up. The term goes back at least as far as the First World War, when a gasper might have been sparked by a lucifer (q.v.). Gasper aside, slang for cigarettes is surprisingly resilient, with 'tabs', 'fags' (late nineteenth century, from 'fag end', a slightly derogatory term for the last of something) and 'smokes' all having a decent lineage, while 'baccy' and 'snout' are well-used terms for the material that goes into making a 'rollie' or filling a pipe. With tobacco, it seems to be the modish 'clever' terms like 'coffin nails' or 'cancer sticks' that quickly fall from favour while the old favourites remain. It is likely, if current anti-tobacco pressures continue, that a whole world of words relating to legitimate smoking may be lost over the next decade, together with the rich folklore of packets (including bizarre myths, like the word 'jew' and the letters 'KKK' on the Marlboro pack, and the supposed naked woman – or man – on the front of the Camel pack). Yet it is also possible that a new clandestine world of outcast tabbers will evolve a rich, fresh vocabulary, one that reflects the changing mores of a society in which the innocent term 'gasper' may now apparently mean someone who enjoys erotic asphyxiation.

Gauleiter

In Nazi Germany, the leader (*Leiter*) of a region (*Gau*). A *Gau* was roughly the equivalent of an English shire, and the archaic German noun was revived by the Nazis and coupled with *Leiter* to describe the political officials given charge of local areas, or the leaders of local branches of the Nazi Party. Whatever the legal authority of a region after Hitler came to power in 1933, the gauleiters, of which there were several different ranks, ran Germany with an unswerving obedience to the Nazi Party line. It was this unquestioning obedience to authority and general willingness to overrule opposition that brought the word to Britain, albeit as an insult. Bosses, council officials, police officers, traffic wardens – basically, anyone deemed to have a modicum of power who was inflexible in the operation of that power, could find himself or herself called a gauleiter or, worse, a 'little Hitler'. (Such people are not a new phenomenon. In Shakespeare's *Measure for Measure*, which dates from 1604, Isabella refers witheringly to 'man, proud man, drest in a little brief authority'.) In view of the evil perpetrated by the Nazis, it was obviously a very wounding insult, though with time it has gently faded from use. Like a great many terms associated with the Nazis, the word is not used in Germany.

Gay

The widespread adoption of 'gay' to mean homosexual – which in its various mutations is both the most popular and the most accepted usage of the word in the English-speaking world today – goes back at least as far as the 1920s. Since the 1970s it has virtually eclipsed all other meanings of the word, from happy and carefree to bright and colourful, even gaudy (not, of course, that these meanings are mutually exclusive). It is, however, worthwhile recording other, now defunct, applications of the word, including the state of being a bit tipsy, and also with reference to an immoral woman or one engaged in prostitution, a 'gay girl' being somewhat akin to a doxy (q.v.) or brass. It was sometimes also deployed as a synonym for lewd or dissolute.

The word offers a very good example of the vibrancy of

the English language, arriving here in the twelfth century from Old French *gai* (although nowadays the French increasingly use *gay* to mean homosexual as well, thus getting their word back, albeit in a different spelling). It had picked up associations of immorality by the seventeenth century when a gay man meant a womanizer. By the 1890s (referred to, mainly in America, as the 'Gay Nineties', and by the upper echelons of English society as the 'Naughty Nineties') the word was still mostly used to mean bright, and it was not until nearly a century later that its primary meaning shifted. Other words have undergone similar transformations – for example, everyone knows that 'nice' once meant fine or subtle (and is still sometimes used in that way), but another former meaning was wanton or profligate, as in this line from Shakespeare's *Antony and Cleopatra* (1606–7): 'For when mine hours were nice and lucky, men did ransom lives of me for jests.'

One occasionally still encounters people who will, often rather pompously, denounce the change in the meaning of gay, but they are fighting a hopeless battle – the meaning is here to stay, at least for the foreseeable future. One interesting difference, though, is that the noun from gay meaning homosexual is 'gayness', whereas that from gay meaning bright or cheerful is 'gaiety'. In *archy and mehitabel* (1927), Don Marquis's wonderful collection of stories about a literate cockroach and a world-weary alley cat, mehitabel the cat often signs off – rather gallantly, given the circumstances of her life – with a cheerful 'toujours gai'.

Gimcrack

A lovely word which, with the proliferation on British high streets of pound stores, remainder bookshops and other outlets for cheap and often poorly designed or made goods, should actually be at the height of its popularity. Gimcrack, which derives originally from a Middle English noun referring to some sort of intricate inlay work, so eventually coming to mean a knick-knack, refers to showy objects – ornaments, gadgets, and so on – of little real use or value, which might alternatively be described as 'gewgaws' (another good Middle English word, though of unknown origin) or even 'tat'. In the past gimcrack goods might have been cheap metal objects, but today they're as likely to be plastic – or even clothing, given the proliferation of ridiculously cheap items pretty much constructed to last until the first visit to the washing machine. In some places (Great Yarmouth springs to mind) entire streets seem to sell nothing but gimcrack (pronounced 'jim-krak'), and it is possible they have been doing so since the word was first adopted in its present meaning in 1676.

Gin and It

This is a mix of gin and Italian vermouth, which to all intents makes it a martini, although today's dry martini is generally made from an equal blend of white (dry) vermouth and gin. The original martini, however, contained four parts sweet red vermouth to one part gin and came garnished with a maraschino cherry. It is this earlier drink that evolved into the gin and It, popular, especially with women, up to, and just beyond, the middle of the twentieth century. Since then the same demographic has been bombarded by Babycham (launched nationally in 1953), seduced by Snowball and pandered to by Pony (both of the latter were 1970s pub staples), before being charmed by Chardonnay in the 1990s. Those remaining stalwarts who still like the taste will today almost certainly ask for a 'sweet martini', which is a shame because 'gin and It' is a far racier name, conjuring up images of saucy baggages (doxy, q.v.) with beehives and loose smiles, offered strong drink by lounge lizards in co-respondent (q.v.) shoes. Sadly, that staple of perhaps a slightly older generation of women, the port and lemon, seems to have disappeared. The great rival to the gin and It, the gin and French, was made with French (dry) vermouth, usually Noilly Prat, to the gin and It's sweet Martini or sweet Cinzano.

Halfpenny, ha'porth

If the bob and the tanner (qq.v.) were affectionately regarded and are remembered fondly, the opposite can be said of the halfpence or halfpenny (pronounced 'hayp'nce' and 'hayp'ny'), the value of which was a ha'porth, a contraction of 'halfpenceworth'. Most of the phrases associated with this copper coin were negative, such as the 'daft ha'porth' of the North of England, used to denote a person who shouldn't be asked to conduct research into rocket propulsion any time soon. Then there is the self-deprecating 'Well, that's my tuppence-ha'porth' to suggest that the opinion offered may not be worth much, since two and a half old pennies – just over one new pence – would not buy a great deal. Similar phrases, like pennyworth, still exist in the UK, as also in the US, where people put in their two cents' worth. The inference is something of little value because the halfpenny wasn't really worth a great deal, and ceased to be legal tender in 1969, when the coin became more expensive to produce than its face value. The Tory MP (Sir) Anthony Beaumont-Dark noted at the time that 'most people don't even bother to pick them up when they drop them.' Running slightly counter to this is the indignant cat in a drawing by Louis Wain asking, 'You call that a ha'porth of milk?', clearly outraged at the small amount in his cup. Then there is the loss to children, unable to go into a shop for a ha'porth of pear drops, or tuppenceworth of halfpenny chews (penny chew, q.v.). Even lower down the financial scale was the farthing, two of which made a halfpenny, so to be without a 'brass farthing' meant to be really very poor. Production of farthings, which date back to the thirteenth century, ended in 1956, and the coin ceased to be legal tender in 1960. With decimalization in 1971, the old coinage began to disappear, to be replaced with 'new pence', of which there was even a 'half penny' or 'half new pee', worth 1.2 old pence, although that too was dropped in 1984.

Ham-and-egg shift

This basically meant the eight-hour day shift from ten to six, usually, though not exclusively, in the mining industry. There has been a strange and ongoing evolution of work terms since the eighteenth century, a time when the *Monty Python* gag about 'working twenty-nine hours a day' would have been lost on many mill owners. Before the Industrial Revolution in the late 1700s and early 1800s, working hours were dictated, far more than is the case today, by the seasons, daylight, saints' days and the weather. Over time Factory Acts, fourteen of them over a one-hundred-and-fifty-year period starting in 1802, regulated hours and improved lighting, which brought the possibility of twenty-four-hour shift working. From the 1860s unions campaigned for the ten-hour and then the eight-hour day, and more recently the target has been a forty-hour week, alongside a great deal being said about the desirability of a better 'work-life balance'. Ironically, the very technology that has enabled flexitime and home working has damaged this balance further by allowing work to bleed into the home space. This does at least mean one can choose meal times, even if ham (fatty meat) and eggs (cholesterol) in the modern diet are frowned on, while the steep decline in heavy industry in Britain since the Second World War has also seen off 'the ham-and-egg shift' as an expression.

Hardtack

Many words and phrases have been lost since the end of conscription into the armed forces with the phasing out of National Service in the UK (it finally ended in 1963), but hardtack belongs primarily to the nautical tradition ('tack' being sailor's slang for food, akin to 'tuck'). Also known as 'sea biscuit' or 'ship's biscuit', it is a hard-baked, flour-based cracker that was cheap to produce and, crucially, could be stored for a long time when other foods might have gone off. A similar type of ration is still used today by those exploring inhospitable environments, but hardtack goes back to the sailors of ancient Egypt and the soldiers of the Roman Empire. There hasn't been too much demand in civilian society for hardtack (which can be dipped in tea to add flavour and soften the biscuit), but if times ever get really difficult economically a batch can be cooked up by mixing flour (two cups), salt (six pinches) and half a cup or so of water. The resultant dough must then be baked for a couple of hours before being cut up into biscuit-sized pieces and baked again.

Heath Robinson

Charming expression for anything that is impractical and eccentric, from ideas and schemes to, most often, designs for products which, if judged sufficiently over-complicated or impractical, are frequently denounced as 'Heath Robinson contraptions'. The term is owed to the illustrator and cartoonist William Heath Robinson (1872–1944), who delighted in sketching unlikely-looking machines designed for highly irregular jobs (rocket-delivered lunch hampers for pilots, for example). His cartoons poked fun at, especially, the supposedly labour-saving inventions that began to proliferate in the early twentieth century, and he specialized in drawing ludicrously over-complicated devices ostensibly designed to perform simple, or even pointless, tasks. Once in common use, 'Heath Robinson' is not much heard now, being largely meaningless to a generation raised on computer games, DVDs and graphic novels.

Here's how!

One of a delightful series of lost, or rarely heard, toasts that includes 'Cheerio!', 'Chin-chin!', 'Bottoms up!' and 'Down the hatch!' Several of these refer to the actions involved in downing, say, a gin and It (q.v.) or other 'short', and may or may not be accompanied by the clinking of glasses together. (It has been said that the original notion behind this was to slop drink between glasses, thus rendering poisoning attempts less effective.) The salutes have largely been replaced by the ubiquitous 'Cheers!', the affected 'Skol!' or ironic variations on 'Mud in your eye!' Perhaps the finest toast of all to have disappeared, or rather to have altered its meaning, is wassail (now usually taken to mean ale or wine mulled with spices), as in the Christmas carol 'Here We

Come A-Wassailing', for which the best-known words date back at least to the seventeenth century, but are probably from much earlier. 'Wassail!' ('Be in [good] health!') is actually the opening part of a Saxon toast – though it may have originated with Danish settlers – to which the reply is 'Drinkhail!' As Bill Bryson explains in *Notes from a Small Island* (1995), this could be repeated until all participants were 'comfortably horizontal'.

High days and holidays

This, which today is a term for special occasions, is to some extent a tautology, in the sense that the word 'holiday' derives from 'holy day', while 'high days' were really just the most important of these religious festivals in the Church calendar – thus the highest holy days are Christmas and Easter, for example. Either way, though, a high day or a holy day meant a break in the regular pattern of daily life, work and worship, and time off from labouring, and so they came to be regarded as special days. Originally some of them would have been the standard national (and international) Church festivals mentioned above, whilst others might have had more local significance (such as Wakes Weeks in Lancashire). Although the word 'holiday' dates from the early Middle Ages, a time when the Church had enormous power and influence over people's lives, today we use it in this sense for bank holidays and other official days off, or to mean a break from work or from some situation, place, or even person. In general speech, high days seem only to survive in the expression, for you never hear someone say 'You realize that Sunday is a high day?' The even more old-fashioned expression 'red-letter day', meaning a day that is going to be or has become special, dates from the eighteenth century and also comes from the Church, from the custom of highlighting festivals on a printed calendar by printing them in red.

Home Service and Light Programme

By as early as 1925 BBC Radio, with its lofty mission to educate, inform and entertain, reached most of the UK. It faced no national competition for nearly seventy years and no (official) local rivals until 1973. Even the unofficial opposition was overcome when the BBC poached the best disc jockeys, including Tony Blackburn and Dave Lee Travis, from offshore pirate radio stations like Radio Caroline. During the preceding decades the BBC's Home Service and Light Programme were listened to by virtually the entire nation. (The more cerebral Third Programme, now BBC Radio Three, was not launched until 1946.) The Light Programme emphasized entertainment although, unlike one of its successors, Radio One, it was not entirely music focused, giving the nation such programmes as *The Archers* (which is still with us, on BBC Radio Four) and *Life with the Lyons*, a 1950s sitcom on both radio and television (which is not).

In 1932 the BBC set up the Empire Service, which became the Overseas Service in November 1939, a few months after the outbreak of the Second World War, when broadcasts were made to Europe; these were taken over by the European Service, which started in 1941. In 1988 the name World Service was adopted for what had become known as BBC External Services, with a remit not so far from George V's first-ever Royal Christmas Message to the Empire, to broadcast to 'men and women, so cut off by the snow, the desert, or the sea, that only voices out of the air can reach them.' It did, and sometimes still does, offer an interesting portrayal of an almost vanished Britain. Programmes that the Home Service, in the form of Radio Four, would not consider broadcasting (Dave Lee Travis's irksomely upbeat *Jolly Good Show*, say) were still being beamed abroad into the twenty-first century.

Both the Home and Overseas Sections of the BBC provided English-speaking people not only with news and topical comment – the first broadcast about the colour bar (q.v.) in Britain was in the 1940s – as well as music of many kinds, drama, comedy and much else besides, but also a large number of catchphrases, some of which remain a vital part of the language. These include 'I don't mind if I do,' 'After you, Claude' and the subsequent Internet message-board favourite 'TTFN' ('Ta-ta for now'). All of those came from Liverpool comedian Tommy Handley (1892–1949), whose own personal catchphrase, 'It's that man again,' has, ironically, vanished. His comedy show of the same title, usually shortened to *ITMA*, ran on the Home Service from 1939 to 1949. It will be interesting to see if many of today's favourites phrases from radio and television have the same reach.

Hugger-mugger

This term, which dates from the sixteenth century, generally means confusion or disorder, but was formerly a word for secrecy, and especially in describing people operating clandestinely together but often in a rather chaotic fashion, so that it is the confusion of action or language that bewilders outsiders as much as the secrecy. Thus to be hugger-mugger with someone meant that you shared their secrets, although often only in a specific area relating to a project or plan.

Like 'hush-hush' or 'on the QT', these rather quaint expressions are being replaced by harsher modern alternatives. However, nothing is as extreme as the latest, and totally unrelated, use of 'hugger-mugger' by the police. They coined it to describe a form of robbery in which an apparently drunk, but jovial, stranger embraces people on the street as a cover for stealing from them.

Indian giver

Offensive and, given the historical facts, rather ironic term for someone who offers a present then asks for his gift back, or who makes it clear that he expects to receive something in return. It belongs in the same category of expressions as 'Dutch treat' or 'Spanish practices', though in this case it is the Native American population that is being insulted. Originally – and unsurprisingly – an American and Canadian term, it dates back to the eighteenth century, and most likely arose because of what might politely be referred to as cultural differences over ownership and trade. Considering how cheaply Europeans acquired the island of Manhattan – said to have been in return for trade goods to the value of sixty Dutch guilders – to pick just one example, it seems only fair that the natives should get a little something back elsewhere.

Invacar

These light-blue, fibreglass-bodied three-wheeled cars, designed for use by the disabled, were once better known by another term which thankfully is now as defunct as the vehicle itself. The first were designed after the Second World War by the motorcycle engineer and designer Bert Greeves (1906–93), who built one for his paralysed cousin and then expanded production to meet the needs of the many disabled servicemen, winning a contract from the government to supply what were then called 'invalid carriages'. Various models were tried but the most popular was Greeves's Invacar, made at Thundersley in Essex, where he also designed and built innovative motorcycles that won considerable success in competition. It was claimed that the Invacar could reach a speed of 60mph, and they were much the most numerous of the designs to be found on Britain's roads; the last was produced in the 1970s. The old DHSS (Department of Health and Social Security, which had succeeded other variously titled ministries involved in the programme) had been funding the production and technically all the cars were owned by the government, as they were leased to drivers as part of their disability benefit.

Their decline was precipitated by other state-inspired mobility schemes and the introduction of new and more stringent safety regulations, and after I April 2003 they were banned from the roads, even though at that point there were only some two hundred left in use. Occasionally one may still spot an Invacar stored amidst other refugees from a previous age, though most were recalled and sent for scrapping. Bert Greeves was appointed MBE for services to the disabled; given that some thousands of his Invacar were produced over more than three decades, providing hitherto undreamed-of mobility and independence to disabled drivers, it seems a rather thin reward. The Greeves motorcycle concern folded in the late 1970s.

Jam sandwich (or jam butty)

Affectionate term, coined in the 1970s and still in use in the 1990s, for a type of police car which was distinguished from the traditional blue 'panda' patrol cars by being both larger and faster, and by having a fluorescent-red horizontal stripe running along its sides, sandwiched between the white of the rest of the vehicle. There is less differentiation between types of police vehicle today as any might be called on to engage in the type of rapid-response work that was formerly the preserve of the jam butty. Oddly, perhaps, there seems to be no equivalent slang term in wide use today, despite the obvious Battenberg-cake markings of modern police vehicles.

Jerrycan (sometimes jerrican)

A steel container for fuel originally designed in Germany – where it was called the *Wehrmachtskanister*, meaning, loosely, 'armed-forces container' – in the 1930s, and stockpiled secretly in the run-up to the Second World War. They were stronger, and easier to handle and pour liquid from, than alternatives used by the British and American forces, and as a result they were soon copied by both major Allied powers. In a nod to the original design these copies were known as 'jerrycans' after the nickname 'jerry' (Boche, q.v.) for a German. Current versions are more likely to be made of plastic, but their shape and size owe everything else to the German originals, even if they are no longer referred to as jerrycans.

Joey

A very good example, perhaps, of one use of a word hastening the end of another. In the aftermath of a 1975 BBC TV *Horizon* documentary, called *Joey*, about Joseph Deacon (a man born with severe cerebral palsy and other conditions) arose the unfortunate use of the term 'joey' to describe anyone with a (perceived) physical or mental handicap. (Joey Deacon died in 1981, aged sixty-one.) The term, along with the equally offensive non-medical use of 'spastic', which had gone well beyond the realm of playground insult, did not survive the different political climate of the 1990s. By then, however, it had certainly banished the other once-common use of 'joey' to mean a clown. This had derived from the famous English clown Joseph Grimaldi (1778–1837), whose character, Joey, is regarded as the first modern clown. Grimaldi is remembered every year at the Clown's Church, All Saints' in Dalston, in Hackney, East London, and his ghost is said to haunt more spots in London than any other spectre, except possibly Winston Churchill's. Grimaldi was also responsible for introducing the dame to pantomime, as well as the idea of audience participation in a show.

Knickerbockers

Knee breeches (also called 'knickers' in the US): a sort of loose-fitting trouser gathered in at the knee or, sometimes, the calf, and once extensively worn by schoolboys and sportsmen, including skiers and mountaineers. Stylized versions are still worn by golfers (very baggy ones are called 'plus-fours', less baggy 'plus-twos', from the extra width in inches) and baseball players, and some British private schools still retain them as part of the uniform, though they are rarely referred to by their proper name. The New York Knicks basketball team does not wear them, but the side's name derives from a nineteenth-century nickname for a New

Yorker. Both this and knickerbockers owe their names to the same source: a satirical work by the American writer Washington Irving (1783–1859) entitled *A History of New York from the Beginning of the World to the End of the Dutch Dynasty*, supposedly by a Dutchman named Diedrich Knickerbocker and first published in 1809. As a result, 'Knickerbocker' came to be used as a nickname for any American descended from Dutch settlers, of which there were many in New York, and hence by extension for a New Yorker – and, ultimately, the Knicks. It is thought that the knee breeches gained the nickname from the illustrations in Irving's book, many of which depicted Dutchmen wearing them. Today, the word's only widespread use in Britain is as part of the name of a rather complex ice cream, the Knickerbocker Glory. The garment itself is still widely worn by walkers (especially on the Continent) and field sportsmen, though generally referred to as 'breeches' (pronounced 'britches') or 'breeks'.

Lascar

A sailor from India (or other eastern countries) employed on European ships over the past five hundred years. The word derives from the Persian *laskar*, meaning army, which in the seventeenth century the Portuguese adapted to *lascari* to refer to an Asian soldier or sailor. The English term lascar, referring specifically to men serving on ships, often under extremely harsh contracts, came from this. The Navigation Acts of 1660 attempted to restrict the number of Asian sailors on any given ship to one third of the full complement of crew, but these strictures were abandoned in subsequent years. The Honourable East India Company recruited seamen from the Gulf and India, and from the nineteenth century on a number of these established small settlements in several ports and cities in Britain. With the decline in British shipping and the Empire, as well as its slightly negative connotations, the word has gently slipped away, although it is found in, for instance, several of Joseph Conrad's novels, and forms part of the title of Rozina Visram's 1986 study, *Ayahs, Lascars and Princes: Indians in Britain 1700–1947*, while Spike Milligan's immortal comic novel *Puckoon* (1963) mentions a 'one-eyed Lascar from a coaling ship in Belfast'.

Liberty bodice

Trade name of an undergarment for women invented towards the end of the nineteenth century and known in America as an 'emancipation waist'. The clue to its function lies in the name, for the Liberty bodice offered the kind of freedom of movement denied by the corset and other Victorian underwear. The Liberty bodice was a sleeveless vest-like garment usually made of warm fabric, sometimes quilted, and often accompanied by suspenders to which stockings could be attached. The bodices, which remained on sale until the 1970s, and were worn especially by young girls, had no extra support built into them, unlike corsets. They derived from the Victorian dress-reform movement that wanted to liberate women from restrictive corsetry and excessive layers of underclothing. Parts of the manifesto of the Rational Dress Society (1881) might ring true today, as it railed against 'any fashion in dress that deforms the figure, impedes the movements of the body, or in any way tends to injure the health. It protests against the wearing of tightly fitting corsets; of high-heeled shoes; of heavily-weighted skirts.' Science backed up the claims of the campaigners for more 'rational' clothing, and in time women's underwear became simpler and less confining.

Although Liberty bodices were originally targeted at lower-class women, especially the servant classes, the lofty aim behind them was to promote women's health through participation in sports (by allowing much freer movement of the upper body), while alerting the public to some of the dangers of, for example, wearing corsets during pregnancy. There is no doubt that it lived up to its name, and that much of what the Rational Dress Society desired has come about. Some of the claims of clothing manufacturers and designers were more questionable, however. The German naturalist and physiologist Gustav Jäger (1832–1917) alleged that only clothing made of animal hair, such as wool, promoted vitality. In 1884 an Englishman named Lewis Tomalin opened a clothes shop in London named, in honour of Jäger and his theories (and with suitable Anglicization of the spelling), Dr Jaeger's Sanitary Woollen System. Tomalin, who had translated Jäger's work, and his descendants did rather well out of it – Jaeger became, and remains, an iconic British brand.

Lily-livered

Generally used to mean cowardly (or sometimes weak or timid), based on the medieval notion that the liver was the seat of courage; other terms include white- or, as Shakespeare has Hamlet describe himself, pigeon-livered. So if one's liver was pale like a lily then clearly one was deficient in blood and therefore, following the medieval logic, lacking in full-blooded courage. The term is not much used now, not least because to call someone lily-livered is a considerable insult, while its close partner, 'yellow-bellied', has long since been reduced to plain 'yellow'.

Lord Haw-Haw

Most commonly associated with William Joyce (1906–46), the nickname was also used more generally to describe anyone from the Allied side involved with pro-Nazi propaganda on the wireless (q.v.) in the Second World War. The most famous programme, titled *Germany Calling* after its opening line, was broadcast in English on the medium-wave station Reichssender Hamburg, and by shortwave to the United States. It started in 1939 and continued until 30 April 1945, when the British Army overran Hamburg.

The programmes attempted to discourage and demoralize British, Commonwealth and American troops, as well as the civilian population of, in particular, Britain, with exaggerated claims of German successes and Allied defeats. They also offered news of the fate of friends and relations who had been captured or who had not returned from bombing raids over Germany, which resulted in an audience made up in large part of those desperate to find out what had happened to their loved ones. The phrase originated in the *Daily Express*, where Joyce's voice was described as speaking 'English of the haw-haw, dammit-get-out-of-my-way variety'. Besides Joyce (who was actually born in America to an English mother and an Irish father, and who, as an ardent supporter of fascism, fled Britain for Germany just before the war to escape detention), there was Wolf Mittler (a German national with a British education) and Norman Baillie-Stewart (a cashiered former officer of the Seaforth Highlanders). Baillie-Stewart served five years in jail while Joyce was tried and eventually hanged for treason, though his wife Margaret (Lady Haw-Haw) escaped prosecution. Many who lived through the war and can remember his broadcasts found that Joyce's clear, mocking tones were among the worst indignities they had to endure.

LSD

Before lysergic acid diethylamide was a slightly scary glint in Timothy Leary's eye, £sd (pronounced, and sometimes written, 'l.s.d.') was a common term for the British currency, sterling. The abbreviation stood for pounds, shillings and pence and originated from the initial letters of the Latin names for three Roman coins, the *libra*, *solidus* and *denarius*.

This non-decimal system, with its tanners and bobs (qq.v.), meant that there were 240 pennies in the pound, which was made up of 20 shillings each containing 12 pennies. The system was based on the currency of the Roman Empire, and can be seen, historically speaking, in the pre-Napoleonic French and other abandoned currencies of Europe. With the emergence of the drug LSD in the 1960s, the opportunity for double entendre was too good to miss, one example being a 1966 single by the Pretty Things called '£SD', but decimalization of the British currency in 1971 eventually did for the expression as applied to money.

Lucifer

As Boy Scouts know, the best thing for lighting a fire in the woods is a dry box of matches, but early examples of these, including the lucifer, had harmful side-effects. Samuel Jones perfected the friction match, invented in the 1820s by John Walker, whereby a mixture of chemicals would ignite if the head of the match was struck or rubbed against a rough surface. (*Lucifer* is the Latin word for 'light-bringing'; it was also, of course, a common name for the Devil, who had originally been the Light-Bringer or 'Light-bringing morning star' before his fall.) Refinements continued through the nineteenth and into the twentieth century, including the addition of white phosphorus, which reduced the pungent smell of the early matches. So by the First World War smokers were happily singing along to George Asaf's famous song from 1915, 'Pack Up Your Troubles', which contains the lines: 'While you've a lucifer to light your fag / Smile boys, that's the style.'

Unfortunately, the use of white (and later yellow) phosphorus resulted in the horribly dangerous and disfiguring side-effect known as 'phossy jaw' and other bone disorders among workers in match factories, and also caused brain damage. From the late 1880s the Salvation Army led campaigns against the use of these chemicals in matches, and even produced its own brand of matches using the far safer red phosphorus; unsurprisingly, these were not called lucifers. Their campaign culminated in a law that prohibited the use of yellow phosphorus after 1910.

Lyons Corner Houses

For many children of the twentieth century a day out in London was not complete without a visit to one of the three Lyons Corner Houses in the West End. These were substantial buildings of up to five floors offering several restaurants, each with a live orchestra, as well as hairdressing salons, telephone booths, theatre-booking agencies and a magnificent food hall. (For those with aspirations the Corner Houses had two upmarket sister restaurants called Maison Lyons, also in central London.)

The British company J. Lyons & Co., founded in 1887, was at one time a huge empire, its core business being in food, catering and hotels, though in the 1950s it founded an innovative and successful electronics arm, which designed and manufactured computers (LEO – Lyons Electronic Office). The company's 200 or so tea shops (the first opened in 1894, the last closed in 1981) were the most recognizable and popular part of the business, notable for their interior

design and, until after the end of the Second World War, smartly uniformed staff (Nippy, q.v.). In 1973 the tea shops were remarketed as Jolyon Restaurants.

Later on the company expanded to include Steak Houses, Wimpy's and Dunkin' Donuts and merged with Allied Brewery in 1978 to form Allied Lyons. In the late 1980s the constituent parts, including Lyons Maid ice cream, were sold off. Of all the varied products Lyons dabbled in, from tea to toothpaste and humbugs to hotels, it may be the tea shops – genteel, friendly places where it was hard to imagine anything really bad happening – that most will miss. Many Lyons products, however, live on, mostly under other names, while the tea shops and Corner Houses survive as fond memories.

Magic lantern

The forerunner of the slide projector, the magic lantern projected images on to a screen or other flat, vertical surface by means of an arrangement of mirrors and a light source, often an oil lamp, with a lens to focus the image. The use of light and glass (or other transparent material) to project images lasted long beyond the arrival of photography and film; indeed photography greatly expanded the number of available images. Neither a film nor a slide projector, however, can quite replicate the eerie flickering of the magic lantern, which, from its development in the seventeenth century, was quickly put to frightening uses with the horror shows, known as 'phantasmagorias', of Revolutionary

France. In these, images might often be projected on to smoke to enhance the spooky effect, and in 'The Casting of the Runes' (1911) the ghost-story writer M. R. James wrote of a particularly devilish display designed to scare children out of their wits, since it featured what appeared to be a real demon. One of the earliest descriptions of the magic lantern, at least in Europe, came from Italy in the mid-sixteenth century, though magic-lantern shows reached the peak of their popularity in Victorian Britain three hundred years later, where patriotic as well as thrilling entertainments featuring a progression of slides amused children (and adults) of all classes. They could not compete with the cinema, however, and, went the way of the machines themselves, which are now collectors' items.

Matinee idol

These belong to a bygone age of weepies and B-movies in which many people, perhaps a majority, watched their films at the local flicks (q.v.) in the afternoon. In a pre-television era, when fewer women worked outside the home, cinemas enjoyed far larger daytime attendances than they do now, which might account for why the term was applied almost exclusively to male stars. Several of these acquired insanely devoted followings, and some briefly entered the language in their own right (the expression 'to be in like Flynn', meaning to act swiftly or impetuously, to seize an opportunity, refers to Errol Flynn), whilst others were never true film stars but occupied a role akin to actors in today's afternoon soaps. Their heyday was from the 1930s to the 1950s, and the use of the phrase began to die out as cinema-watching habits changed, especially after television became widespread, although you may still hear someone described as having 'matinee-idol looks'. The more general modern term 'movie star' covers a far broader spectrum of actors, from big screen to home cinema, as well as encompassing both sexes.

Milk bars

Although there are still a few remaining, including a number of Willie Griffiths's National Milk Bars, the idea of fashionable youth congregating in milk bars has vanished, as has the use of the phrase as a generic term rather than to indicate a specific venue. Griffiths opened his first in 1933 in Colwyn Bay and at its peak his empire stretched to seventeen in Wales and bordering English counties. Other chains and one-offs spread across the whole country – by 1936 there were more than 1,000 milk bars – and their popularity gave rise to the famous Korova Milk Bar in Antony Burgess's *A Clockwork Orange* (1962), which in turn inspired the cult New York nightclub of the same name founded in the 1980s. It is, however, unlikely that Mr Griffiths, originally a dairy farmer from mid-Wales, would have approved of the substances sold at either of those, and any milk and cream they might have sold certainly did not come from his farm at Forden. In the milk bar's heyday there was even a National Milk Bar in Liverpool's Lime Street station to greet Welsh Beatles fans with a taste of home, which was frequented by the band themselves, and it was in Liverpool this century that attempts were made by council leader Warren Bradley to turn boarded-up pubs into twenty-first-century milk bars for the city's youth.

Mods and Rockers

There are still 'Mod' nights in Brighton today, and it appears to be one of those rare subculture words that will remain with us. 'Rocker', too, looks like sticking around, although its meaning has shifted away from motorbike-riding 'greasers' simply to mean someone who likes rock music. What has, perhaps thankfully, departed is the notion of Mods and Rockers going toe-to-toe (aggro, q.v.) on the seafronts of Britain.

The phenomenon first occurred in the 1960s, with swarms of young people descending on motor scooters (parka-wearing Mods) or motorbikes (leather-clad Rockers) on South Coast resorts like Brighton, Bournemouth and Margate. Since the two groups' tastes in everything from means of transport to clothes to music were almost diametrically opposed, it should not have been a great surprise when they clashed, sometimes violently. It was in Margate, one May bank holiday weekend in 1964, that the local magistrate told the offending invaders they were 'unkempt, mentally unstable, petty little sawdust Caesars who can only find courage by hunting in packs like rats.' Similar tear-ups occurred in the Mod revival of the early 1980s but since then the idea of Mods and Rockers has become rather quaint, and it's hard to believe that they had once inspired so much panic, anger and soul-searching, fuelled by the almost hysterical reactions of the media. They also inspired Stanley Cohen's 1972 classic of sociology, *Folk Devils and Moral Panics*, in which the author states that moral panic (a term he coined) occurs when a 'condition, episode, person or group of persons emerges to become defined as a threat to societal values and interests'. His work was developed by Geoffrey Pearson in *Hooligan: A History of Respectable Fears* (1983). Both these books point out that youth gangs are neither a new, nor a revolutionary phenomenon in the British Isles, and both should perhaps be required reading for headline writers today.

Mrs Grundy

Best known now as a character in *The Archers*, the only surviving wireless (q.v.) entertainment show from the BBC Light Programme (Home Service and Light Programme, q.v.). In her previous incarnation, however, Mrs Grundy is a character alluded to, but not actually present, in a play called *Speed the Plough* by Thomas Morton (?1764–1838), first performed in 1798. This makes her almost unique in literature in becoming such a well-known figure (representing conventionality, prudishness and, oddly, since she pre-dates the reign of Victoria by four decades, Victorian morality) without actually 'existing' as a character, although Morton's play often alludes to her with the question 'What would Mrs Grundy say?', which became a popular catchphrase. She is, however, a magnificent cipher, and as such is mentioned by Thackeray, Dickens, John Stuart Mill, Dostoyevsky, G. K. Chesterton and James Joyce, amongst others. She is cited in just about any work on English propriety or prudery, and yet today has been erased by a wife from rural Middle England, which, happily, is pretty much how the original Mrs Grundy started life. In the modern world, however, even the Grundys cannot appear too old-fashioned, which is why the current arbiters of English probity have buried the Mrs Grundy of the television age (Whitehouse, Mary, q.v.) in a very deep hole.

Mufti

Like many other words (for instance dekko, q.v.), this is another casualty of the end of the Empire, though most people would recognize the synonym 'civvies' to describe everyday clothes worn by someone who is more accustomed to a uniform. *Mufti* is an Arabic word for an expert in Islamic law and quite how it came to mean casual clothing in Britain is anyone's guess; the idea offered by *Brewer's Dictionary of Phrase and Fable* is that the robes and cap of the Muslim lawman were not dissimilar to those of off-duty British soldiers serving in the Middle East. Children in British schools are sometimes offered a 'mufti day', usually a Friday on which they are allowed to wear their own clothes rather than school uniform, often in return for a small donation to some worthy cause selected by the school. It is rare now, however, to hear someone say 'I was in mufti at the time,' or 'Because he was off duty at the time, PC Bigelow was in mufti.'

Never in a month of Sundays

A long or emphatic way of saying 'never', this is a phrase that has lost its purpose now that the British Sunday has become so much more like any other day. Laws lifting restrictions on trading and pub hours, among other legislation, as well as the shifting of major events to the Sabbath, means that the dismal options which, in 1988, Morrissey sang about in 'Everyday Is Like Sunday' have improved and expanded beyond measure. Oddly, though, this short-lived later meaning of a month of Sundays as something ineffably drab superseded an earlier one of it as something to celebrate; free time away from work when a person had all the time in the world. So to fail to do something even in the course of an entire month of Sundays meant, pretty much, that it would never get done, for that was considered a huge amount of spare time. The earliest known printed reference to the phrase is from 1759 in the *Life and Real Adventures of Hamilton Murray, written by himself*, giving it 250 years of usage, or an awful lot of Sundays.

Nice as ninepence, As

This is the exception to all those other (often pejorative) phrases like 'as bent as a nine-bob note' (bob, q.v.) in that a ninepence coin did once exist (there was, for instance, a silver one issued in the early nineteenth century), although there is no indication that the coins were particularly nice or 'neat' (the other chief variation of the phrase). It would appear that the expression is all about the alliteration, which is possibly why some sources have suggested that it derives from 'as neat as ninepins', ninepins being the traditional form of skittles (Not all beer and skittles, q.v.). However, the phrase 'As fine as fivepence, as neat as ninepence' can be traced to the seventeenth century, so its continuation into the twenty-first isn't a bad innings.

Nippy

The first waitresses in the tea shops and restaurants established and run by J. Lyons and Co. were known as 'Gladyses', but in the 1920s they were superseded by Nippies, who also staffed the restaurants in the Lyons Corner Houses (q.v.). The nickname was apparently inspired by the quick and neat motions needed to serve customers in a crowded eatery. The Nippy – who wore a black uniform, like a maid's, with white collar and cuffs and a white apron, topped by a curious black-and-white cap not unlike a cloth tiara – became a national icon whose wholesome and proper

image was strictly maintained, though in an interesting example of changing social mores a range of Nippy gaspers (q.v.) was briefly introduced. Children could dress up as mini-Nippies in outfits bought by indulgent parents, and in the early 1930s a musical called *Nippy* enjoyed a successful run; there was even a pack of playing cards in which the queens were Nippies. One child who never grew up to be Nippy, however, much though she might have wished to, was Margaret (now Baroness) Thatcher. Instead she worked at the Hammersmith headquarters of J. Lyons as a research chemist, and during her time there she was part of the team that invented the ice cream Mr Whippy.

Nit nurse

A victim of more enlightened times and health campaigns that now spare children being inspected in public by a stranger and then being sent home from school with a pink letter and a prescription for Derbac. Although head lice in schoolchildren have not gone away, Nitty Nora the nit nurse has become a figure of folklore, along with Parkie the park keeper and other semi-official authority figures from childhood who, although often disliked, did at least offer children a strand of adult supervision that was neither parent nor teacher.

None of your beeswax

A delightfully meaningless (unless you are involved in apiculture) way of advising someone to keep their nose out of other people's affairs (nosy parker, q.v.). Despite all manner of pseudo derivations to do with the use of beeswax in make-up in centuries past, and thus the meaning that a lady should attend to her own face not others', the real origin appears to be a more pleasant way of saying 'mind your own business' based on a jokey similarity in sound of the words 'business' and 'beeswax', and was popularized in the 1930s. A continued request for information might result in a further riposte of 'Not on your Nellie!' which essentially means 'No chance' or, literally, 'Not on your life', from the slightly convoluted rhyming slang 'Nellie Duff' for 'puff', an old-fashioned slang word for 'life'. 'Did you ever in your puff see such a perfect perisher!' exclaims Bertie Wooster in P. G. Wodehouse's immortal *The Code of the Woosters* (1938).

Nosy parker

'Now I go cleanin' windows to earn an honest bob, / For a nosy parker it's an interestin' job,' as George Formby sang in his 1936 hit 'When I'm Cleaning Windows'. This lovely, and declining, rather than lost, term says much about the British. No one likes a nosy parker, which is what makes Formby's refreshing admission such a good lyric. Being nosy has long been synonymous with inquisitiveness, and *Brewer's Dictionary of Phrase and Fable* argues that the term derives originally from someone who pokes their nose in, a 'nosy poker'. A more specific, if tenuous, derivation comes from Eric Partridge's *Dictionary of Slang and Unconventional English* (1937 and subsequently), which suggests a link to the prurient ways of the royal park keepers supervising the 1851 Great Exhibition. The *Oxford Dictionary of English*, however, confidently asserts that it comes from an early twentieth-century postcard caption, 'The Adventures of Nosey Parker', about a peeping Tom in London's Hyde Park. Other unlikely notions include derivation from the inquisitorial ways of Matthew Parker, Archbishop of Canterbury under Mary I and then Elizabeth I, or even from the inquisitive ways of the rabbit, for which 'parker' is an archaic term.

As George Orwell wrote in his 1941 essay 'England Your

England', 'the most hateful of all names in an English ear is nosy parker. It is obvious, of course, that even this purely private liberty is a lost cause. Like all other modern people, the English are in process of being numbered, labelled, conscripted, "co-ordinated".' He was writing of the Nazi threat to this country, but in this context professional snooping, whether through CCTV or e-mail monitoring, thrives in the modern world of data-theft scares, with the result that the amateur curtain-twitcher has been left rather out on a limb.

Not all beer and skittles

Skittles or ninepins is still played in some pubs in England and Wales, and there are actually local Skittles Leagues, but it is nothing like as popular as it once was. It dates back to at least the seventeenth century and is a simple game involving wooden pins set up in a diamond pattern with players throwing a ball at them to knock them down. The expression was usually employed to contrast a coming period of difficulty with the pleasures of a careless afternoon in the boozer. Dickens in *The Pickwick Papers* (1837) introduced a variant, 'It's a reg'lar holiday to them – all porter and skittles' (porter being a dark brown bitter made from charred or browned malt). The expression has declined with the popularity of skittles and has been supplanted by phrases like 'It's hardly a picnic,' 'It's no stroll in the woods' or 'It's not a piece of cake.'

Oojah

One of a number of very useful words ('thingamabob' or 'thingummy' is another; an American might prefer 'doohickey') which can literally refer to anything at all that a person has temporarily or permanently forgotten, or does not wish to mention by name. In *Right Ho, Jeeves* (1934), P. G. Wodehouse's second full-length novel about the inimitable valet, Bertie Wooster tells his Aunt Dahlia that 'things are not looking too oojah-cum-spiff at the moment.' The expression dates from earlier, however, and was, if not actually created by the British Army, certainly popularized by the troops and in that way spread across the world and into everyday speech. A *Washington Post* article from 1917 (resurrected by the Lost for Words blogspot) shows the ambivalent relationship of 'proper writers' to these slang terms entering the language and the writer's uncertainty that he was doing the correct thing in mentioning them, as that would only spread them further. Referring to oojah, he wrote:

> Heaven forbid that I should perpetuate such a monument of silliness; but, indeed, I fear that the rhyming slang fashion is all too deeply established: our recruits are carrying it far and wide, and its entry into the civilian language will be one of the least satisfactory souvenirs of Armageddon.

In this case his fears were unjustified, for oojah has fallen rather short of Doomsday.

Ottoman

This deeply useful, and functional, household item has fallen victim to the Scandinavian-design-led home-decoration revolution since the 1980s. Probably French, rather than Turkish, in origin, it takes its name not from its invention by Ottoman Turks but from their supposed habit of lounging around on such furniture. Essentially a backless padded seat, it could be sofa- or pouffe-sized, with smaller ones often serving as footstools. In some the padded top was hinged and could be lifted up to provide storage underneath, thereby maximizing space. However, heavy furnishings, particularly those which completely conceal stored items, are frowned upon in the modern home, being considered bad feng shui. This is in itself notable, as feng shui itself dropped out of fashion with such rapidity that it would surely be a candidate itself for any future edition of this book.

Parade

In this sense, not a public procession or military display, but a public square, promenade or row of shops. The first of these two meanings has long since disappeared, but the concept of the parade of shops lingered into the modern era. A parade would usually just be a short row of retailers on one side of the street only, often set back a little to allow parking, and traditionally consisted of local stores serving the immediate community and some passing trade. Shops might include butchers, grocers, pharmacists, hairdressers, newsagents, a florist and very often something completely off the wall that had just sort of ended up there, such as a specialist hobby shop, travel agent or artificial-limb stockist. The grander parades might include a small post office or a sub-branch of a bank or building society.

At least, that was the way things were. In the past there might, in one in four parades, have been a chippy, whereas now some form of fast-food outlet is a given. As indeed are estate agents, a small supermarket and a diminishing selection of the previous stalwarts, except for hairdressers, who continue to be over-represented. The decline of parades as convenient shopping areas for local people has been largely because of the rise of bigger supermarkets, changing eating habits and the fracturing of communities, as well as the inability of small shops to offer the long opening hours that people require in the twenty-first century.

The term came into its own with the suburban developments of first the 1920s and then the 1950s, well before the notion of the drive to the 'hypermarket', a word which, oddly enough, has itself disappeared. At least within the UK no one talks of hypermarkets, but in the new expatriate colonies of the Spanish Costas the word is still used. That's one of the beauties of English – a word that the British had the merest dalliance with for a few years in the seventies and eighties goes abroad and, linguistically, makes its fortune. No doubt at some point in the future it'll return, looking leathery but fit, to mainstream English, just as so many other words have in the past.

Parthian shot

The return of this rather attractive term would be a welcome addition to the language, although over the last half-century it has been all but obliterated by the similar-sounding and meaning, but technically incorrect, 'parting shot'. A Parthian, or indeed parting, shot is the last word, a frequently barbed, pithy or telling remark with no chance for the recipient to come back. The point is obvious if one says 'parting shot' because that is a point of separation, but there is a much more interesting history to the Parthian variant. It alludes to the practice of the Parthian horsemen (the kingdom of Parthia is now part of Iran) who were trained to ride their horses hands-free. In battle the cavalry would fake a retreat before swivelling in their saddles and firing arrows at their pursuers. It made for a devastating final statement, which is of course the aim of any valedictory comment.

Pell-mell

Chaotic, helter-skelter, higgledy-piggledy or jumbled would be good alternatives here, but any description of disorderly or reckless haste would do. It derives in part from French *mêler*, to mix, but, perhaps appropriately in view of its meaning, it has origins in another foreign word, Italian *pallamaglio*, which translates as ball-mallet, to confuse the issue. This referred to paille-maille (or pall-mall, among other spellings), an early form of croquet played in the pre-Georgian era by London's nobility and gentry in the area around what is now St James's Street. From this we get the street name Pall Mall, which is situated at the southern end of St James's Street – apparently the matches were end-to-end stuff, although whether that accounts for the meaning of haste and disorder is not known. The use of pell-mell as an adjective is now rare, although not so rare as the original but long-vanished game.

Penny chew

There is probably a whole book to be written on lost confectionery and other much-loved comfort food. There is certainly a small industry supplying 'retro' sweets such as Curly Wurlies, Freddo chocolate, Refreshers and Anglo Bubbly bubble gum. These companies also provide some of the key products that would once have come under the heading of penny chews (or even two- or four-for-a-penny chews, costing a halfpenny or a farthing each; *see* Halfpenny, ha'porth), such as Mojos, Black Jacks and Fruit Salad. The main reason that the term 'penny chew' has vanished, however, is not to do with the complete disappearance of the product, but just because inflation has eroded the value of the currency, as the sweets did children's teeth, so that the notion of a penny buying anything has become pretty much redundant. Also redundant, sadly, are many thousands of Woolworths staff who sold the Pic n' Mix range from that now defunct high-street store. These were until recently a key dispenser of some of the delights formerly known as penny chews. In February 2009 the last bag of Woolworths Pic n' Mix sweets was sold on eBay for £14,500, which was donated to charity.

Pin money

There are lots of amusing, if incorrect, theories about the origin of this term, including the notion that it was first used in connection with Henry VIII and gifts he gave to his wives. It originally meant a small amount of money given to a woman by her husband or, sometimes, father, often as an allowance, to be spent on small or non-essential personal items, 'pin' in this case meaning 'a decorative clasp for hair or garment'. It dates from the seventeenth century, and in time came also to mean small sums earned in a part-time job. The important aspect, though, is that it was for 'extra' purchases, rather than necessities. While some women would cheerfully admit to doing a job for pin money, the term came to be used pejoratively in the period after the Second World War, when it was argued that men, and especially those returning to civilian life from the armed services, should be employed ahead of women. This carried the implication that all women only worked for pin money, while men needed a proper income to support a woman, amongst other things. The term is not much heard now, possibly because it has also been used as an argument to justify the difference in pay scales between men and women doing the same job.

Pithead ballot

This phrase was one of a whole raft of trade-union related terms that have either disappeared or are on the verge of doing so, and seems to have left the language after the battle fought by the government against the National Union of Mineworkers in the 1980s. 'Collective bargaining', 'show of hands', 'flying picket' and 'closed shop', like 'pithead ballot', all belong to the era when trade unions had some real influence and industrial unrest was common. One barely hears the word 'solidarity' used in the context of workers' rights any more, and outside of the old mining communities, where memories of the bitter strike of 1984 to 1985 linger, even the deadly insult 'scab' – meaning a strike breaker – has gone. The American writer Jack London

(1876–1916) wrote a 250-word definition of a scab, one of the more affectionate parts of which runs:

> A scab is a two-legged animal with a cork-screw soul, a water-logged brain, a combination backbone of jelly and glue. Where others have hearts, he carries a tumour of rotten principles.

Poodlefaker

Quite gorgeously bonkers word for a young man, often a newly commissioned officer, who habitually socializes with women. There is little apparent logic to its derivation until one learns that 'poodle' was nineteenth-century army slang for a woman, and 'faker' in this context refers to pretend emotions. (An alternative derivation is that the person is playing the role of a lap dog.) It refers, almost always disparagingly, to a man who cultivates the company of women for his own ends, whether these were social advancement, appearance or, less often, directly financial. George Orwell offers a glimpse of the dim view taken of poodlefakers in his novel *Burmese Days* (1934), when describing a kind of British officer who censoriously viewed any social duties at all as poodlefaking, and who disapproved of women in general: 'In his view they were a kind of siren whose one aim was to lure men away from polo and enmesh them in tea fights and tennis-parties.' Perhaps the last widely reported use of the word in public was in the early part of this century when Tony Blair was described by Boris Johnson, in an article in the *Daily Telegraph*, as a 'mincing poodlefaker'.

There is something slightly effeminate, or at least faux-effeminate, about the poodlefaker, possibly because of the word's association with poodles, and it is a trait he shares with the 'fancy man', another term seldom heard these days. The latter was often held up in a poor light against the honest toiling chap, but this was partly because he could court the ladies with his fast car, flash clothes and 'smart talk'. The fancy man (or woman, for that matter) was also considered too flighty to be marriage material, though he might break up a few, but offered a welcome break from the often drab lives of women stuck at home. Some fellows might refer to them disparagingly as 'ponces', and a few fancy men may indeed have been procurers for prostitution, but most were just flash blokes after fast times.

Pooh-pooh

A way of fairly politely, but firmly, dismissing an idea or pretty much anything else, it derives from the repetition of a nonsense sound, 'pooh', suggestive of impatience, scorn or contempt, and originally of disgust. It has no clear relationship to the equally defunct term 'pooh-bah' or 'grand pooh-bah', so called from the self-important character in Gilbert and Sullivan's comic opera *The Mikado* (1885). The satirical use of pooh-bah to describe anyone with an overly high opinion of himself, or fond of awarding himself titles (it is almost always a male), has gone, but the word litters popular culture of the recent past, including the American cartoon show *The Flintstones*. 'Pooh-pooh', however, is still sometimes heard, but usually with the implication that whatever has been pooh-poohed may not have been given a fair hearing.

Pop (bottle of)

The simple description is of a carbonated drink that does not contain alcohol, although the term was sometimes broadened to include cordials, squashes and other non-alcoholic beverages (slightly oddly, since the word is obviously onomatopoeic, from the sound of a bottle of fizz being uncorked). It is the huge expansion in the market for the latter, along with bottled water (something that barely existed in the UK prior to the 1980s), that has finished the word off, the dictionary rather sniffily describing it as 'dated or North American'. Until relatively recently the choice, for a drink to consume on the move, was between a can or bottle of pop or a carton or bottle of milk; still drinks like orange squash were usually mixed at home, and juices were both rare and pricey. The options today, from elderflower presses to high-energy drinks and isotonic waters, mean that people tend to be very specific about which kind of drink they choose. Health concerns have affected sales of pop, but old favourites like cherryade, dandelion and burdock and ginger beer still hang on; until recently Vimto outsold the cola giants in Saudi Arabia, and Irn Bru has achieved a kind of cult status as a hangover cure in Russia.

Portmanteau

In certain specialist areas (including film, pharmacy and mathematics) the word still has some currency to describe several things that make up a whole, but no one in those fields would take a portmanteau to a conference to discuss such matters. In the nineteenth century (and well into the twentieth), however, that was the chief meaning of portmanteau – a large travelling case. Victorian portmanteaus were often vast, large enough for clothes to hang from a rail inside them, but the word was later applied to any large travelling bag, especially one made from stout leather. It is a very simple derivation of French origin from *porter* (to carry) and *manteau* (coat), thus a case or bag in which to carry your coats and, by extension, other items of clothing. A corruption of the term lived on in parts of Australia until the late twentieth century, where school bags were referred to as 'school ports'. The word is also often encountered in the study of the English language, for a 'portmanteau' word (sometimes simply 'portmanteau') is one that combines the sounds and meanings of two words to give a new meaning, such as 'brunch' (breakfast and lunch). The term was invented by Lewis Carroll, who devised many such words himself, including 'slithy' (slimy and lithe) and 'mimsy' (miserable and flimsy); modern examples include 'blaxploitation' (black and exploitation) and Tanzania (the former African countries Tanganyika and Zanzibar).

Pound in your pocket, the

Sounding appropriately modern, this phrase, used by Harold Wilson in a radio and TV broadcast in November 1967, was a response to the devaluation of the pound to US $2.40, an attempt to break the cycle of boom-and-bust economics. Prime Minister Wilson was keen to stress that the drop in value on the international markets would not affect the strength of the pound in the pocket of ordinary Britons. At a time of limited international travel this would certainly have been the case, while the currency restrictions then in place would have insulated the economy further. The full quote ran: 'It [devaluation] does not mean that the pound here in Britain, in your pocket or purse or in your bank, has been devalued.' However, it was a psychological blow at a time when governments set a great deal more store on the value of their currency than is the case now, and the phrase was widely derided; for Wilson, it probably came under the heading 'Things I Wish I Hadn't Said'. It became a political catch phrase, but perhaps because of the odium it attracted, it is usually used nowadays, if at all, in an ironic sense.

Pully hawly

Quite literally, once one gets beyond the spelling, 'to pull and haul', a phrase which, originating in the eighteenth century, meant a sexual encounter. Thus 'a game at pully hawly' was similar to a bit of slap and tickle' or 'a roll in the hay' as a way of referring indirectly to sexual intercourse. The English are traditionally wary of talking openly about sex, which is perhaps why there is such an abundance of euphemistic terms relating to it still current in the language. Whether education programmes and the relatively recent fashion for explicit and open conversations will eventually do away with the euphemisms is unlikely. In part this is because many of the terms are very funny and, as John Cleese once noted, an Englishman would still rather be considered a bad lover than lacking a sense of humour.

Punchcard

Few areas have changed as rapidly as office work, and especially computing, over the past thirty years, which have seen USB flash drives replace CDs , which in turn took over from small disks, which replaced larger floppies, which were akin to the punchcards (or 'punched cards') that for decades had been the means of inputting data into a computer. These cards had patterned holes punched into them representing letters and numbers and which, taken together, built up into a database. Given the speed of technological change nowadays, punchcards have become as obsolete as the primitive computers they served. The expression 'to punch one's card', however, has nothing to do with computers, and simply means putting a card into an automatic time recorder ('punch clock' or 'clock card machine') at the beginning and end of the working day, the machine then stamping the card with the date and the time of beginning and finishing work, a process usually known as 'clocking on' or 'clocking off'.

Puttee

This, sometimes spelled puttie, derives from the Hindi word *patti* (band, bandage) to describe a long strip of cloth wound in such a way as to cover the lower part of the leg from the ankle to the knee. Puttees are wrapped tightly and spirally round the legs to act as support and protection, and as such were often worn by riders or cyclists, although mostly by soldiers. They were a standard part of the uniforms of several armies throughout much of the nineteenth and twentieth centuries, where the requirement that they be wound absolutely evenly occasioned much cursing among the rank and file. The word came into English from soldiers returning from service in India in Victorian times, and like so many terms from Britain's imperial past, its use now is mainly historical.

Quart

This is still a perfectly respectable unit of measurement denoting two imperial pints (or one quarter of a gallon – hence the name), just as a pole (or rod) is five yards and eighteen inches (or sixteen and a half feet) and four of them equate to a chain, ten of which make a furlong, of which eight comprise a statute mile. Despite metrification, the mile is unlikely to disappear from use, and furlong is firmly established among the racing fraternity. The same sort of grasp of the key units will save some imperial measurements such as the pint and possibly the gallon, but the gill (one quarter of a pint or five fluid ounces, also known as a 'noggin'), along with the quart, is pretty much lost, in the way that the chopin (a Scottish unit of liquid measurement roughly equivalent to a quart) has already been.

Just to confuse the issue, the chopin was actually half the old Scottish pint measurement (which was equal to three imperial pints), whereas a quart is two imperial pints – this is possibly what Whitbread had in mind with its 1970s advertising slogan for its Trophy Bitter, 'The pint that thinks it's a quart!' Such jingles often live long after the campaign has finished – which is half their point – so 'Guinness is good for you' has lasted decades, whereas others (such as 'Wouldn't you rather be Hemeling?' 'Follow the bear!' and 'Double Diamond works wonders') have become lost. To confuse matters even further, the US liquid pint, quart and gallon are all smaller than their imperial equivalents... Moreover, since 2000, it has been illegal in the United Kingdom to sell any liquids other than milk (in returnable bottles), beer or cider in pint measures.

Queer Street (to be on)

First use of this of this term – it seems to date from the very early nineteenth century – merely indicated that something was wrong with a person, or that they were suffering from (non-specific) troubles. By the late nineteenth century, however, Queer Street came to have a precise location with a distinct link to financial difficulties – Carey Street, near Lincoln's Inn Fields (Lincoln's Inn being one of London's Inns of Court), where a bankruptcy court was situated. It would appear that the phrases 'to be on Queer Street' and 'to be on Carey Street' merged, and both came to be used to indicate that someone had money problems, although one may still, rarely, hear someone say 'We'll be on Queer Street,' meaning to be in trouble. Another link to the law courts comes via 'queer cuffin', an old nickname for a magistrate which doubled up as a term for a rude or surly person, along with the phrase queer cove (q.v.).

In an odd coincidence, in view of the later use of 'queer' as an offensive term for homosexual, which resulted in the decline of the phrase, the centre of gay London in the Georgian era was at the end of Carey Street, near where the London School of Economics is today. It was also the hub of London's then thriving smut-publishing industry.

Rachmanism

This term came to be used to describe a landlord who exploited his tenants. It derives from the notorious activities of Peter Rachman (1919–62), a West London landlord in the 1950s. Born in Poland and interred during the Second World War by both the Nazis and the Soviets, Rachman went on to fight for the Allies and settled in Britain in 1948. He rapidly built up a property empire consisting of more than a hundred mansion blocks and several nightclubs. His success lay in subdividing his flats for multiple occupancy, and, unlike most landlords of the time, in not operating a colour bar (q.v.); the large West Indian population in the Notting Hill area is a lasting legacy of Rachman. He exploited new immigrants terribly; living conditions were squalid and he employed henchmen to bully his tenants if they failed to keep up their rent payments. In 1963, a year after his death at the age of forty-two, the Profumo scandal broke and it was revealed that both Christine Keeler and Mandy Rice-Davies ('Well he would [say that], wouldn't he?' q.v.) had been Rachman's mistresses, having been set up in a mews house that he owned. The 1965 Rent Act, offering greater protection for tenants, was a direct result of Rachman and his activities.

Radiogram

These huge objects – some were sofa-sized, others a more modest chest-of-drawers scale – were at the peak of their popularity during the 1950s. As its portmanteau (q.v.) name suggests, it was a combined (valve) radio and gramophone (record player) and represented the height of mid-twentieth-century multimedia. The turntable was able to spin a variety of discs, which were mostly made of vinyl: first 78s (because they completed 78 revolutions in a minute), then 45s (45 rpm; also known as 'singles'), which contained a song on either side, EPs (extended-play 45s), and the much larger long-players (LPs, 33⅓ rpm). Radiograms came in all shades of wood-surround from light tropical to Beethoven teak, and would often offer bonus features such as storage space for records or other items. Sophisticated chaps might even use them as a sort of music-playing cocktail bar whilst entertaining at home.

The popularity of radiograms helped to boost record sales, and by the late 1950s discs outstripped sheet music sales for the first time and became (with their later incarnations as cassette tapes and CDs) the chief means of establishing the popularity of a song until the recent download revolution. From this era came a host of phrases teetering on the brink of the linguistic abyss, from 'hit parade' to 'pick of the pops'.

Rapscallion

Rather sweet term for a young man who indulges in mild, often irritating but also amusing, misbehaviour; someone who is a bit of a scamp, but not malicious. 'Scallywag', and even 'ragamuffin', might have also served as synonyms once, but these have mutated into the more criminally minded scally (street arab, q.v.) and the dancehall style of ragga over recent decades. The essential link is still there, at least in the minds of many scallies, who regard their behaviour as rascally good-natured and a bit of a laugh rather than violent, offensive or threatening. The word, which dates from the late seventeenth century, possibly as a humorous adaptation of 'rascal', is now regarded by dictionaries as archaic.

Rot or tommyrot

A chap just doesn't say this sort of thing any more when he means nonsense, yet at one time, depending on the tone of voice employed, it could be a harsh and dismissive rebuke. The modern equivalent is probably 'bullshit' or 'bollocks', both of which have passed out of the swearing paradigm over the past couple of decades – 'bollocks' since the famous 1977 trial involving the Sex Pistols album *Never Mind the Bollocks*, when the High Court upheld one not very convincing interpretation of bollocks as nonsense, particularly that delivered by the clergy. (Perhaps inspired by the innocuous etymology of 'poppycock', which comes from the Dutch *pappy cak*, 'soft shit' – What the dickens!, q.v.)

'Tommyrot' refers originally to soldier's rations (Tommy, q.v.) specifically bread, but the word has come to mean bosh, twaddle or codswallop, words similarly rarely used nowadays. 'Bosh', from a Turkish word meaning empty, gained popularity after the publication of James Justinian Morier's novel *Ayesha the Maid of Kars* (1834). Queen Victoria used it to criticize the proposed plans for Tower Bridge: 'To those who say the bridge will increase the defensive strength of the Tower and improve the beauty and historical associations of the place, all I can say is bosh!' Codswallop can claim no such illustrious pedigree, and despite the best attempts to link it to codpieces and beer (via the still just-used nickname for beer, wallop) is actually first recorded as dating from 1959 in BBC Radio's *Hancock's Half-Hour*.

Rozzer

Term, 'of unknown origin', for a policeman coined in the nineteenth century that disappeared from mainstream use by the twenty-first, but even so managed to outlive other later words such as 'bogey' and 'filth'. Bogey was used to describe any form of investigator or snoop from nosy parkers (q.v.) to landlords, but was most frequently employed to describe detectives. Filth enjoyed brief popularity from the 1960s to the 1980s as a general term for police officer, specifically the London CID, which was hit by a number of bribery and racketeering scandals during this era. 'Bobbies' and 'peelers' (from Sir Robert Peel, 1788–1850, founder of the Metropolitan Police), 'plod', 'fuzz', and 'Sweeney' (from 'Sweeney Todd', rhyming slang for Flying Squad) have all come and (largely) gone; 'pigs' is just another American verbal import like the more current 'feds' or 'five-oh'. Today the most popular slang terms tend to be regional rather than national, though most people would understand references to the 'Old Bill', 'bizzies' or 'dibble'.

Rubber Johnny

This is a very rare example of an extremely popular slang or informal term being supplanted by the correct word. The widespread promotion, and advertising, of condoms in the 1980s as protection against AIDS, in particular, meant that jokier terms like rubber Johnny, which dates from the 1960s, or earlier euphemisms such as 'French letter' fell out of favour. Interestingly, the French slang for condom is 'English bonnet'. (As an aside, French farmers, often bicycle mounted, who brought their produce over to Britain were known as 'onion Johnnies'. This practice largely died out in the 1950s but was once quite large scale, with over 9,000 tons cycled around the UK in 1929 alone.)

Returning to the rubber variety, the more widespread availability of this form of contraception also put paid to the non-ironic use of the euphemistic question employed by barbers, 'Something for the weekend sir?' The condom moved out of the hairdressers and into just about everywhere, collecting new flavours, textures and colours as it went. They became a fashion item, special holsters were designed for holding them and they are practically obligatory at certain gatherings. This has removed much of the embarrassment associated with purchasing them and is excellent news for rubber-producing countries. It also means that schoolchildren called John, Johnson or Jonathan are spared the classroom request 'Can I borrow your rubber, Johnny?', and adaptations of 'The Clapping Song' (originally a hit for Shirley Ellis in the 1960s) which switched the words 'rubber dolly' to 'rubber Johnny' have disappeared.

Rules OK

Interesting but short-lived bit of phraseology and graffiti that has vanished in its original incarnation as a yob (q.v.) manifesto, but which is still used as a punning title for articles about rules. The key difference between 'Street End

Aggro [q.v.] Rules OK' and 'Fiscal Rules OK?' is not the question mark but the meaning of rules. In the first the word rules is being used as a synonym for reigns, whereas in the second it means a code of laws or guidelines. Very occasionally one might see something like 'Rovers Rule OK?' but this isn't using OK in the sense of 'If that's all right with the rest of you;' rather, it is a sort of anti-question stating a fact and daring anyone to oppose or contradict it. An exclamation mark might have been more appropriate, but for some reason these were never employed. The addition of OK and a question mark to a statement is a particularly 1970s convention, when it was also attached to the suggestion that George Davies is innocent as part of the (false) claim that he had been fitted up by the filth (rozzer, q.v.). Of the many jokey variants, 'Elizabeth II Rules UK' is one of the cleverer.

Rum

Very often used almost in admiration as much as in warning, prefixing anything with 'rum', meaning curious, peculiar or eccentric, indicated that the listener should pay attention to the person or event being talked about. Originating in the eighteenth century, and unrelated to the cane sugar- or molasses-based liquor, its early use indicated excellence, while later the meaning shifts closer to 'strange'. The 1811 edition of Francis Grose's *A Classical Dictionary of the Vulgar Tongue* has dozens of definitions of words prefixed by 'rum', from rum cove (qq.v.) – a dextrous and clever rogue – to rum doxy (q.v.) – a beautiful woman. By the twentieth century this multiple use had been pared back to indicate that a person might be a bit of a handful ('A rum 'un, that,' similar to 'He's a wrong 'un, and his father was a wrong 'un too'). 'A rum situation' might be used to describe a tight spot or odd occurrence, especially one that the speaker had not come across before. Today the word is chiefly used either ironically or facetiously, which is a pity, as it conveys a little more than mere oddness.

Running-board

On early cars up to the late 1950s (and even later for some models), a kind of footboard running down each side just below the doors, typically extending from the front to the rear mudguard. A rare item today, this side of retro cars or people who wish to make some sort of statement about their individuality. SUVs have a truncated step that is similar, but in the past few cars were complete without a running board to aid ingress and egress, as well as to provide dramatic shots in gangster films. The ornate running-board has been used for purely aesthetic effect as well, and there have been various revivals in America. There is no doubt that they attract show-offs, so much so that the highway codes of most countries have a section about not riding on the running-board. Since modern mass-produced cars with their monocoque body shells have no mudguards, these elegant additions have become redundant.

Sawbones

Delightful old term for doctor, or more accurately a surgeon, which most people will only be familiar with through the truncated version on *Star Trek*, where the ship's doctor is referred to as Leonard 'Bones' McCoy. First noted in 1837, it is quite simply the splicing together of the word 'saw' with 'bones', but today is only used jocularly, like the even older 'quack doctor', usually reduced to plain 'quack'.

Serge

Along with other trappings of more military eras the recognizable twill fabric (with ridges on both sides) has rather fallen from favour. Although the word is derived from the Latin *sericus*, silken, via French, there is now a softer, finer variety known as French serge, and silk serge (used for linings) is widely seen but rarely mentioned outside the clothing industry. The heavier worsted sort of serge is still sometimes used in making military uniforms and trench coats which, post-war, pretty much every male possessed. This is no longer the case since the end of National Service and the change in menswear fashion in favour of denim, which, ironically, has a similar weave and is thought to derive from a shortening of *serge de Nîmes*.

Shanks's mare or Shanks's pony (to go by)

A quaint way of saying walking, the shank being the shin or area of the leg below the knee. The slogan was rather nicely used during the Second World War to suggest that people should walk when they could to save resources, the official posters showing a happy pony with a shoe covering most of its torso trotting along cheerily.

Shindy

Slightly archaic term for ruckus, quarrel, affray or bit of biff. There are dozens of semi-retired terms for fighting in the English language, but as a traditionally violent nation we seem reluctant to let go of set-to, rumpus, scrimmage, tussle, brawl or barney, despite the availability of fisticuffs, scrap, tear-up and exchange of blows.

Sire

Though relatively recently still used of animals, in particular horses, nobody 'sires' children today, and the words begat or procreate look to be on the danger list too. It is a gloriously aristocratic word and that may be the reason for its decline, as the only person it might be appropriate for would be some roaring patriarch in breeches declaring to his assembled family 'I have sired the future generations of this family,' before adding in an undertone, 'and several others too.' The word goes back at least to Jacobean times, as evidenced by a line in Shakespeare's *Cymbeline* (1609–10): 'Cowards father cowards and base things sire base.'

Slide rule

The slide rule itself still exists, but its practical use has been seriously curtailed by the increase in availability of computers from the 1950s onwards, and even more so by cheap calculators since the 1970s. Some pocket-sized scientific calculators were even known as 'slide-rule calculators' and were able rapidly to replicate the computations and readings that slide rules had been necessary for since the seventeenth century. For centuries, therefore, they were indispensable as mathematical aids, and running a slide rule over something was a final and rigorous test of the validity of any theory or proposition.

Spend a penny

At one time this was a highly descriptive euphemism for going to the toilet, because for more than a hundred years visiting a public lavatory actually cost one (old) penny (0.4p), since the doors were opened by dropping a penny in a slot in the lock, then turning the handle. This gradually became less and less widespread with the coming of decimalization in 1971, as the replacement of literally thousands of toilet doors across the country to accommodate the new currency was beyond the reach of most local councils. Previous inertia was the reason why the phrase remained around for much of the twentieth century, as the cost of visiting a 'public convenience' had remained static for so long. With the advent of automated coin-in-the-slot toilets and others, as at stations, entered via coin-operated turnstiles the cost of 'spending a penny' has now risen to twenty, thirty or even fifty pence in some places (50p = 120 old pence …).

Spirit duplicator

These were also known as 'Banda' or 'Ditto' machines, the former term being most prevalent in the UK. Prior to the widespread use of the first photocopiers, these machines offered schools, churches and small political groups a cheap and easy means of duplicating information. The name derives from the alcohols which were a major component of the solvents used in these machines. Material to be duplicated was written or typed on to special two-ply sheets of paper (cheerily named 'spirit masters'), one of which was pre-coated with a layer of wax that had been impregnated with a colorant. The pressure of writing or typing on the top sheet transferred coloured wax to its underside, producing a reverse image of the desired marks. The first sheet was then fastened on to the drum of the machine, with the waxed side out. As the paper moved through the printer, a solvent spread across each new sheet of paper would dissolve just enough of the pigmented wax to produce a copy. Usually the resultant 'print offs' were a dim purple on cheap paper that retained the smell of the solvent, and it is this scent that most will remember for enlivening dull school lessons with its intoxicating aroma. Indeed, the harmful effects of sniffing one's notes led to an early discontinuation of use in some areas. (*See also* Xerox.)

Spooning

This is still used to describe a sleeping (or, indeed, lovemaking) position where one person holds another closely from behind so they fit together like two spoons. It no longer refers, however, to kissing or canoodling or making out, or any of the other myriad words for the clothed embraces of lovers, a meaning that survived certainly until the Second World War. It could also mean to court (courting, q.v.) someone, often in an unbearably sentimental fashion, and this is very probably the route by which, in the nineteenth century, 'spoon' acquired its association with kissing. There was an older meaning of spoon to describe a silly sort of brainless person, and spooning was often used dismissively of young lovers to imply that their heads were empty of anything else but necking, snogging, and so on.

Sport

'She bought her own car and got in with the Brighton sports, thinks she's too good for the likes of us now,' sniffs the young taxi driver at the beginning of Ian Fleming's *Thunderball* (1961). He was referring to a local doxy (q.v.) who had done well for herself, but the use of 'sports' to describe racy young men with a bit of money didn't last much beyond the next wave of fashionable young men on the Brighton Road (Mods and Rockers, q.v.). The sports were a product of the mass motoring age and replaced the 'swells' of an earlier era. They could be from any background, though most were working-class boys who had seized the opportunities of a new economy: blokes with a bit of money who enjoyed life's racier pleasures. The phrase 'Go on, be a sport!', which is still heard today, touches on the same unstuffy approach to life and morals.

Sputnik

One of a handful of Russian words that have entered mainstream English, but also a word and a concept whose time has passed. *Sputnik*, literally 'travelling companion', is

Russian for satellite, and during the space race and science-fiction boom of the 1950s and early sixties carried with it dreams of adventure and travel beyond the stars. It also excited the United States government, which was terrified, after the successful launch on 4 October 1957 of Sputnik I – the first manmade satellite to orbit the earth – that America might lose space to the Soviet Union. Sputnik 2 was launched the following month, carrying the ill-fated Laika, a stray dog that had the dubious honour of being the first animal to be sent out into orbit. More sputniks were sent into space, more or less successfully, over the next few years, culminating in the successful manned space flight with Yuri Gagarin in April 1961.

The Soviet lead was not to last (though in 1963 they were the first to send a woman, Valentina Tereshkova, into space):

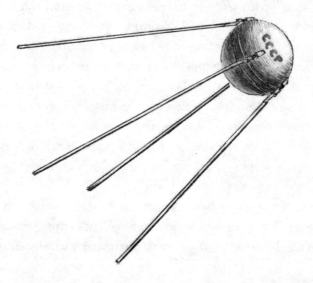

America soon caught up and eventually overtook the Soviet Union in space exploration, and in 1962 became involved in the public–private partnership (as it would be called today) that was Telstar. This first communications satellite carrying broadcast and telecommunications signals was a collaborative effort between NASA, several US telecommunications firms, the GPO (as the Post Office then was) in Britain and the French national post office. Later Sputnik missions were failures and not widely broadcast. More recently, in 1997, Sputnik 40, a model of Sputnik I, was launched from space station *Mir* to mark the fortieth anniversary of the first mission.

Stamps and coupons

George Orwell noted that coupon snipping is one of the defining characteristics of the English. The word comes from French *couper*, to cut, and has the sense of a printed form offering the holder free or discounted goods, or other benefit. Coupons still hang on through Internet promotions, though 'voucher' tends to be the more widely used term, and the popularity of loyalty cards and air miles has further eroded the once mighty coupon, which were for so long a regular feature of newspapers and magazines. Government-issued coupons were also a vital feature of life during the Second World War (and, for some items, until nearly ten years after it ended), since they regulated a person's ability to buy rationed items such as food, clothing and petrol. Stamps as a means of saving only survive in very poor areas, whereas once

Green Shield Stamps, in particular – a kind of early loyalty scheme to reward shoppers, introduced in 1958 – were very popular until they were withdrawn in the early 1990s. The genius of stamps from a business point of view is that during inflationary times they decrease in value; further, as founder Richard Tompkins discovered, many were never cashed in.

Both coupons and stamps have shifted from being a part of everyone's lives to an existence on the margins and, despite economic fluctuations, are unlikely to re-emerge in their previous forms, not least because of the proliferation of retail loyalty-card schemes.

Street Arab

It is not hard to see why this term to describe semi-vagrant street urchins has fallen from use. However for Dickens, Conan Doyle and other writers the term meant any children, often orphans, who lived on the streets of Britain's cities. The modern equivalent might be 'hoodie', 'herbert' or 'scally' (rapscallion, q.v.), all of which refer to semi-feral urban youths who challenge orthodox notions of dress, manners and social order, or at least are said by the yellow press (q.v.) to do so. The term was most popular in the nineteenth century but survived up until the time when wider society recognized separate youth groups with their own designations, such as 'punks' or 'skinheads'. Lee Jackson's *A Dictionary of Victorian London* (2006) offers the following observation of a typical street Arab (from *Punch*, 1842):

He has a shrewdness of observation, a precocious cunning, and, above all, an art of annoying ... We confess, that for all our usually placid disposition, when walking in the streets we cannot stand the sarcasms of the little boys. They are like mosquitoes, who sting and buzz about you, but are never to be caught.

Street cred

In the age of *Pop Idol* the concept seems almost quaint, and the term is heardly heard nowadays. The mania for street credibility reached its peak in the late 1970s during the punk era, and was to some extent tied to those more class-conscious times. Despite the involvement of large numbers of middle-class art students, punk liked to portray itself as a working-class sub-culture. Also as part of its DIY ethos, displaying the trappings of the previous era's bloated superstardom status was frowned upon. No Elvis, Beatles or Rolling Stones in 1977, as The Clash sang.

Elvis did literally die that year, and street cred became the watchword. The best definition of it came from the late cartoonist Ray Lowry (1944–2008), who said that 'street credibility is the ability to change the tyre on your tour van in your stage clothes on the Old Kent Road without getting beaten up.' Maintaining the appearance of street credibility was also important commercially, because bands that lacked it, or were perceived as 'selling out', would rapidly dwindle in popularity. It was important because punk affected, and to a certain extent did actually possess, an ideology – or as John Lydon, otherwise Johnny Rotten of The Sex Pistols, said at the time, 'We mean it, maaaaan.'

Student power

This carries the notion of power being a liberating force, best wielded by those on the margins, students, schoolchildren or whichever other group might improve the world by seizing control. (At least, that is what former Spice Girl Geri Halliwell meant by 'girl power'.) Today, however, the whole idea of student radicalism in the UK has become very last-century, and the phrase is now one of a series of slogans from the 1960s counter-culture that have been chanted for the last time, or which are only employed ironically when quoting the Trotskyite Wolfie ('Freedom for Tooting!') Smith, from the late-1970s TV sitcom *Citizen Smith*.

Tanner

Of all the 'lost' coins of the realm the tanner – the use of the word dates from the early nineteenth century, though its origin is unknown – or sixpence is possibly the most missed. First struck in 1551 (with the head of Edward VI on them), they lasted 420 years until decimalization in 1971. Then their value was rather rudely dropped from half a shilling to two and half new pence, though they remained legal tender at this new (de)value until 1980. Up until 1920 they were pure silver, and half silver till 1946, though this did not stop their addition to Christmas puddings post-war as a 'lucky' gift.

This linking with luck is perhaps due to the coin's longevity, and for much of the post-war period many footballers carried sixpences in their boots, while a bride might be given one on her wedding day. The association of luck, love and tanners did not hold true for everyone, however, least of all the greatest siren of the British goggle-box, Elsie Tanner of ITV's long-running soap, *Coronation Street*. This northern bint (doxy, q.v.) was already looking out of place by the 1970s, and disappeared from public view four years after the coin she was named for.

To boot

This is scarcely ever ever heard today without an accompanying thigh slap, usually by the principal boy in a pantomime. It quite simply means 'in addition to', and derives from the Old English *bot* meaning 'advantage' or 'remedy'. Whether this is what the 'boots' (bootboys) once provided in hotels by polishing guests' shoes is another issue, but such staff are no longer referred to by the term.

Although 'to boot' has nothing to do with footwear, with this age of trainers and its corresponding decline in the wearing of more formal shoes has come a similar fall in the use of shoe-based metaphors. To be 'down at heel' is still sometimes heard, although few people realize the direct relationship between a person's worn-down footwear and their financial situation. The same is true of the far less used 'on one's uppers', which refers to the sole being virtually entirely worn away, leaving only the upper part of the shoe left.

Toilet

A much used word in the context of going to the lavatory, but a lost one when it comes to its former primary meaning – as in 'to attend to one's toilet' – of grooming or preparing oneself for the day, or evening, ahead. There is even an archaic use of the word to refer to a dressing table, though the actual derivation is from the French word *toile*, meaning a piece of cloth on which were placed items connected with grooming, such as hairbrushes. Sherlock Holmes would often use the state of a person and whether they had neglected their toilet as a means of gauging the likely seriousness of a client. People still attend to their toilet, but refer to shaving, washing, putting on make-up and all the other functions of assembling oneself for the outside world by other terms.

Tommy

Colloquial word for a British soldier, it comes from 'Thomas Atkins', which was adopted in the early nineteenth century as a specimen name appearing on official Army forms. It is especially associated with the First World War, when it was used by German soldiers as well as Allied troops, just as Jerry

(Boche q.v.), GI (government issue) and Charlie came to be used to describe German, American and Vietcong troops respectively. Although 'Tommies' could refer to British troops in general, singular 'Tommy' invariably means a private soldier, the honest and slightly put-upon working-class troops that have always formed the Army's backbone. Kipling, in his poem 'Tommy' (1892), noted how differently these young men are treated in peacetime compared to when there's fighting to be done:

> I went into a public-'ouse to get a pint o' beer,
> The publican 'e up an' sez, 'We serve no red-
>   coats here.'
> The girls be'ind the bar they laughed an' giggled
>   fit to die,
> I outs into the street again an' to myself sez I:
> O it's Tommy this, an' Tommy that, an' 'Tommy,
>   go away';
> But it's 'Thank you, Mister Atkins,' when the
>   band begins to play.

In this he was only echoing something soldiers have quietly put up with for centuries, and continue to do so.

Tonic

Used to describe anything that revitalizes a person mentally, physically or emotionally, yet tends now to be employed only in very specific senses medicinally (or, in another meaning, musically), or for the quinine-based mixer that frequently accompanies gin. The general use of a certain kind of drink as a bracer or pick-me-up has largely disappeared, but essentially all the modern high-energy, vitamin-rich, naturally sourced concoctions are just a new variant on the old sarsaparilla and other enliveners from the past. The other use of the word that has gone is the notion of a person being such a cheery soul that they act as a tonic for those around them. In fact, the only popular modern use of tonic in this sense is, disturbingly, the phrase 'a tonic for the troops,' and that largely seems to have survived because it was the title of an album (1978) by Irish band The Boomtown Rats, fronted by (Sir) Bob Geldolf.

Touch of the tar brush

Derogatory, if euphemistic, British slang expression for anyone thought to have black or Asian ancestry. A less offensive term today would be 'mixed race', but actually that would miss the nuance of the phrase, which was originally used about anyone with dark looks, regardless of his or her racial heritage. It basically implied that somewhere that person's ancestry included descent from someone of a different race, which in port cities such as Bristol, Cardiff and Liverpool was extremely likely. Indeed, a 1991 documentary film by John Akomfrah called *Touch of the Tar Brush* examined the impact of what today would be called multiculturalism in Liverpool.

Another odd and now defunct word for dark-skinned was 'Dixie' (after the nickname for the Southern United States), which, according to one theory, led to English football's greatest goal scorer, William Ralph Dean of Everton, being better known as Dixie Dean. This word, like 'coloured', has mostly fallen out of use, as has 'touch of the tar brush'.

Trolleybus

Essentially, trackless trams, often double-deckers, powered by overhead electricity cables, the current being picked up by an articulated trolley pole (or poles) on the vehicle's roof. A nice example of a word that has been lost but may, if the plans of Leeds City Council come off, soon return both to the city streets and the lips of English speakers in the UK. Although common across Europe and in parts of America and Canada, trolleybuses were once widespread in the UK, with fifty systems operating across the country; however, the last of them – in Bradford – were decommissioned in 1972. They were as much a part of the urban British scene as trams and Routemaster buses, and that chronicler of bygone transport, John Betjeman, gives them a glancing mention in his poem 'Business Girls':

> Rest you there, poor unbelov'd ones,
> Lap your loneliness in heat.
> All too soon the tiny breakfast,
> Trolley-bus and windy street!

Tube

Not only has this nickname for television largely vanished, but the technology that gave rise to the term has also been almost completely overtaken. The cathode-ray tube made possible the appearance of images on a screen, and until the development of cheap liquid-crystal display and plasma screens, was the main means of showing broadcast and other images on a television set. In America it also gave rise to the term 'boob tube' for TV, the inference being that watching too much of it turned you into one. Since 'boob' has a different meaning in Britain, the terms most commonly used here were 'idiot box' or 'goggle box'.

Ironically, these were coined and most frequently used at a time when, by today's standards, a decent proportion of TV output would not have caused the viewer to consider self-harm or hard drugs as viable alternative forms of entertainment. Yet the truth is that television has always had good and bad shows – it's just that today there is more TV, and correspondingly, therefore, more poor programmes available to viewers. Television is mostly, after all, commercially driven, and thus naturally follows Gresham's Law that bad money drives out good, or in this case *Big Brother* drives out big drama. The nickname also provided the title of a ground-breaking, if anarchic, music programme on Channel 4 from the early 1980s, which launched the television careers of, amongst others, Paula Yates and Terry Christian.

Tumblers

As a form of entertainment, tumbling just doesn't cut it any more. At least, no one seems to refer to acrobats by that name nowadays, although tumbling remains one of the disciplines within gymnastics, and requires much the same coordination, balance, strength and agility as other acrobatics. Gymnastics aside, tumbling is still part of a clown's (Joey, q.v.) repertoire, but today the child's party that offers tumblers as a special attraction is likely to be thinly attended. After all, if one wants to see grown men fall over for no good reason there is plenty of televised football.

Other circus or traditional country-fair entertainments have disappeared, from catching the greasy pig to climbing the greasy pole. This is largely because of changing tastes and, in some cases, such as freak shows, greater sensitivity, but the seemingly oxymoronic, modern trend towards resurrecting traditional arts and festivities, coupled with the mania for rebranding, may yet see 'tumblaerobics' as the next weight-loss sensation.

Tussie-mussie

A small posy of flowers which is either carried by a bridesmaid at a wedding, or pinned to her dress by means of a small decorative vase. Dating from medieval times, the word appears to derive from the earlier 'tussemose', related to more familiar 'tussock', and until well into the Victorian era it could also mean a bunch of aromatic herbs carried to disguise unpleasant smells, in the days before 'personal hygiene'. It's an odd, if pleasing sounding, way of referring to a bouquet, but is probably only used by florists nowadays. It is, however, no odder or older than many other wedding traditions, some of which date back centuries with little alteration.

U and Non-U

It is a modern conceit to suggest that class no longer exists in the United Kingdom, but it is now rare for it to be defined through the speech gradations U and non-U. 'U' in this context stands for upper class, and it first surfaced in 1956 in a scholarly article by a Professor Alan Ross. The 'non-U' he referred to was the everyday speech of the aspirant middle classes of the post-war period. It was part of a broader debate about social class, but came to be most focused on vocabulary and pronunciation, in particular whether one used certain telling words such as napkin or serviette, graveyard or cemetery, pudding or sweet. By the time Nancy Mitford and others picked up on the term, publishing an amusing and bestselling book called *Noblesse Oblige: An Enquiry into the Identifiable Characteristics of the English Aristocracy* based upon Ross's article, the nation's chattering classes were checking each other's natter for giveaway clues, starting a debate about class-consciousness and snobbery that rumbled on into the 1970s. Even today, though rarely, someone may describe something as being 'rather non-U'. Possibly the neatest explanation of the phenomenon was provided by John Betjeman in his poem 'How To Get On In Society', which in five succinct verses delivers over thirty fatal linguistic and social errors. There are seven in this verse, from the putting of milk in before the tea to the pronunciation of 'scones' to rhyme with 'stones', as well as the use of non-U words like preserve and doileys.

> Milk and then just as it comes, dear?
> I'm afraid the preserve's full of stones;
> Beg pardon, I'm soiling the doileys
> With afternoon tea-cakes and scones.

UB40

Best known in respect of the Midlands band, who adopted it as their name because they met while they were unemployed and the Unemployment Benefit Form 40 was as good a way as any of expressing their condition. As the old Labour Exchanges gave way to Job Centres, so the forms by which benefits are delivered have changed, and UB40 is now known as the Job Seekers' Allowance. The whole area of benefits is replete with (if you'll pardon the pun) redundant terms, including the YTS (Youth Training Schemes) and YOP (Youth Opportunity Programmes), some of which sank without trace whilst others lingered longer in the language; one still occasionally hears a young and lowly paid recent recruit to a company referred to as 'the YTS kid'. Other terms for the unemployed come in and out of vogue, from the rhyming slang 'rock and roll' (for 'on the dole') to 'being on the social', 'going to scratch', 'signing on' or 'getting the giro'. The last few are unlikely ever to leave the language because they have entered that magical repository of folksong and tradition, the football chant.

Vapours (an attack of the)

Used to describe any number of mental or emotional conditions, from depression and hysteria to mood swings and fainting. Today these would all be segmented off into their proper ghettos of bi-polar or pre-menstrual tension, rather than be collectively put down to vapours or its synonym, nerves. The latter word was deployed much more broadly in the past to describe a character or way of being, and 'a fit of nerves' was used very often to describe 'female complaints'. Today 'the vapours' is mainly used jocularly, to describe someone getting in a bit of a tizzy.

Veranda

This is an external (but often, or even usually, roofed) gallery area attached to one or more sides of a house which offered shade and shelter, and in hot climates would be cooler than the interior. It derives from Portuguese *varanda*, meaning a railing or balustrade, though it originally came from Hindi, like so many other terms in English that are still used (such as bungalow) or which have all but disappeared (dekko, q.v.). A veranda (or verandah) is generally raised above ground level, perhaps partly to improve the view from the seats that are often to be found on them. Warm climates like India or Portugal, or even parts of the United States, lend themselves to this architectural feature, but they are rare in the UK, hence the decline in the use of the word.

Washing boards

A wooden board with ridges on it that was used in conjunction with (or occasionally instead of) a dolly (q.v.), it was particularly good for stubborn stains which could be removed by rubbing the fabric against the board's uneven surface. Whether the cloth was then passed on to the wash tub and dolly or just rinsed, it would eventually have to be wrung out and dried. This drying process was aided by using a mangle, which consisted of two rollers through which the laundry was passed by turning a handle. Later versions were electric but initially mangles were hand-operated and, like the dolly, required a good deal of strength to operate for any length of time. The disappearance of washing boards was inevitable once washing machines became widespread.

Wayfarer

A simple, if now rather quaint, term from the Old English word *faran*, to travel, and 'way' in the sense of a track or road, meaning to make one's own way on foot. It conjures an image of someone travelling at a gentle untroubled pace with no particular need to arrive at any time. This makes it antithetical to the modern world of fast travel and appointment-driven journeying, though unlike other terms connected with walking – the noun 'tramp', for example – it has not been stigmatized. The closest modern synonym might be 'rambler', but even they have an element of urgency about them.

Well, he would [say that], wouldn't he?

A heavily used catchphrase that arose from the Profumo scandal of 1963 (Rachmanism, q.v.). It is a quote from one of the principal characters, Mandy Rice-Davies, at the trial of another, Stephen Ward, which arose from the denial by Lord Astor that he had had an affair with her. Many urban legends surround the scandal, which involved government ministers and foreign spies, as well as the nobility. The yellow press (q.v.) had a field day and as a result all kinds of possibly apocryphal stories were reported, including the alleged first words of the Malaysian Prime Minister on arrival in London, which were quoted as 'I want Mandi.' The fact that *mandi* in Malay means to take a shower or bath was explained in less bold type.

The scandal broke the Macmillan government, which was thrown out of office a year later, and heralded the official beginning of Swinging London; it was noted, in passing, by the poet Philip Larkin, who wrote:

> Sexual intercourse began
> In nineteen sixty-three
> (which was rather late for me) –

The phrase came to be used whenever someone wished to cast doubt on the truth of a comment, and lasted rather longer than Miss Rice-Davies's fame – after a failed pop career, she described her life as 'one slow descent into respectability'.

What the dickens!

One could also be given the dickens for, say, a late arrival or other misdemeanour, or have the dickens of a time finding something that was difficult to reach. 'What the dickens,' however, was a general term of surprise similar to 'What the deuce' – both words standing in for 'the Devil' (even though 'deuce' does sound rather like the French word *Dieu*, God). 'The deuce!' is often used to express anger. The earliest known written instance of dickens ('devilkins') is in Shakespeare's *The Merry Wives of Windsor* (1597): 'I cannot tell what the dickens his name is.' So the phrase has nothing to do with the Victorian novelist, and indeed predates him by several centuries.

Expressions like this are 'minced oaths', deriving from an age when polite and/or God-fearing people *did* mince their words. There are many more, from 'By Jove' (substituting a Roman deity for God) to 'Strewth' (God's truth), most of which have fallen into disuse as it became broadly acceptable to take in vain the names of God, Jesus or the Devil. A few, like 'Cor blimey' (supposedly from 'God blind me') or 'Tarnation' (from 'Damnation' used as an oath), 'Crikey' and 'Cripes' (from Christ), are still just hanging on (as does 'Strewth' in Australia), whereas it's safe to say that 'Zounds' (God's wounds) and 'Odds bodkins' (God's body) have definitely strayed off the linguistic map. (*See also* Rot or tommyrot.)

Whitehouse, Mary

A Christian campaigner who died in 2001, most famous for her attacks on the broadcast and other media which she saw as undermining the nation's morals. She was the founder of the National Viewers' and Listeners' Association, which lives on as Mediawatch. Originally an art teacher, in the early 1960s she became responsible for sex education at a secondary school. It was perhaps her shocked reaction to some of her pupils' morals, for which she blamed television, that started her off. She began her 'Clean Up TV' campaign in 1963 and by 1965 had collected over half a million signatures for a petition sent to the Queen. Although many of her legal actions failed it would appear she did influence future laws about the broadcasting of warning signs on films, and had a pornographic magazine named in her honour to go with the CBE to which she was appointed in 1980.

Her own favourite programmes were *Dixon of Dock Green*, *Neighbours*, and coverage of snooker, while she had issues with *Till Death Us Do Part*, *Monty Python's Flying Circus*, *Not the Nine O'Clock News*, the swearing in *Four Weddings and a Funeral* – and *Doctor Who* (for its 'nightmarish qualities'). This earned her a place in pop culture, not only in the programmes she targeted, but also in the BBC radio and TV topical comedy show *The Mary Whitehouse Experience* (1989–92), while she was one of the influences behind Mrs Merton in the spoof television chat show *The Mrs Merton Show* (1994–8). This latter character perhaps captured the wit, humour and charm of the real Mary Whitehouse, although many others in the media probably shared the views of the comedian Bernard Manning, who said, 'She'll be sadly missed, I imagine, but not by me.' (*See also* Mrs Grundy.)

Wireless

This was a very sensible and widely used term for radio communications in the days before mobile phones and the Internet. It referred to a radio transmitter or receiver, which for most people just meant their wireless set or radiogram (q.v.) at home, on which they might listen to the Home Service (q.v.), Lord Haw-Haw (q.v.) during the war, or any number of other programmes. As the technology moved from valve to transistor (a word which itself has dropped from the language) to digital, and batteries improved, receivers could be made smaller and more portable. 'The wireless' has proved a surprisingly durable form of communication with more broadcasters using the technology via the Internet, so making a mockery of the 1979 Buggles hit 'Video Killed the Radio Star'. By then, however, the word 'wireless' was already regarded as the preserve of the elderly and fogeyish (it was also thought by some to be more upper-class than 'radio' – *see* U and non-U), evoking images of the whole family sitting around a set listening to Vera Lynn, rather than younger people with their transistors and earpieces or terrifying 'ghetto blasters', or, most vexing of all, the coffee-swilling world netizen looking for a hot spot for his laptop. The word has enjoyed a slight revival, however, in the term 'wireless broadband'.

Wizard

It is ironic that a time which has seen the greatest ever worldwide interest in wizards and witches coincided with the disappearance of the word 'wizard' to express delight or congratulations. It is a nice piece of irony that the boy wizard Harry Potter and his school chums are unable to use this word in the context in which it was most favoured in the boarding-school story tradition (the *Mallory Towers* or *Just William* books, for example), which J. K. Rowling draws on. It is unlikely that, satirical use aside, we shall ever hear someone shout 'Wizard scheme, Melissa!', or a young girl describe her father as 'the wizardest daddy on earth'.

Wizard is one of many lost terms to express pleasure, including the short-lived 'goody goody gumdrops', which first appeared, ironically for such a British-sounding term, in an American cartoon in the 1930s. Indeed, although wizard is considered British slang, its first recorded use seems to be in the American novelist Sinclair Lewis's *Babbitt* (1922). *The Wizard* was also the name of a popular boys' comic that ran from 1922 to 1963, when it merged with *The Rover*.

Woolton Pie

This was exactly the sort of thing the wartime Ministry of Information had in mind when it produced the slogan 'Better pot luck with Churchill today than humble pie with Hitler tomorrow.' The pie was an attempt to produce something tasty and nutritious during wartime rationing. Chefs at the Savoy Hotel came up with the recipe and it was named for the Minister of Food, Lord Woolton (1883–1964), following, ironically, the same sort of guidelines the government is trying to impose on school meals today.

The recipe varied over the seasons, but Woolton Pie was basically a medley of root vegetables, including potatoes, carrots, swedes, parsnips and, for the fortunate, maybe a bit of turnip. Oats and chopped onions were added to the stock the vegetables were boiled in before being covered with pastry and grated cheese. It is, like scouse (from lobscouse, a kind of stew often eaten on ships as its ingredients were variable and could be stored for a long time; hence its association with ports and, in particular, Liverpool), a good basic food for people operating on a low budget.

Wrong side of the blanket (to be born on the)

Put simply, this is an old-fashioned euphemism for 'bastard'. Before the Child Support Agency and today's much more tolerant attitude towards single-parent families, illegitimacy carried far greater stigma, but although the phrase implies that the child has not been not born into any family (and until well into the twentieth century many were sent for adoption or to orphanages), that may not always have been the case. The expression may equally refer to a child whose mother and father were married, but to other people. The key point, however, is that a child born on the wrong side of the blanket is born away from the father's home or to an unmarried mother, and was denied any legitimate claims to an inheritance.

Some noble families sidestepped this issue by prefixing the father's forename with 'Fitz-', which had formerly denoted any son, to refer to illegitimate male offspring. In this way the son of William Jones, say, would not inherit the name Jones but might be known by the surname Fitzwilliam. All in all, however, it was better to be born on the wrong side of any blanket than to have been 'born to be hanged', although this did apparently mean one was immune from death by drowning.

Xerox

According to the official definition, Xerox is a global document-management company which once hit the Hooveresque heights of having its name associated with its chief product. So well known was the company for supplying photocopiers that the verb 'to xerox' was widely used as a synonym for photocopying. That time has gone and the rightful verb has returned, but Xerox can be proud not only of the company's previous hegemony when it came to copying documents, but also in producing one of the few items of office furniture (other than the telephone) to have a song written about it ('Zerox' [*sic*] by Adam and the Ants, 1981).

Yellow press

It is perhaps odd that the phrase 'yellow journalism', first used in America in 1895, has fallen out of use, because we live in a golden age of exactly that. The term, from 'yellow kid journalism' after a popular comic strip of the day, describes a type of reporting which aims to increase circulation through eye-catching headlines and a deliberate avoidance of serious news, unless a 'human interest' or celebrity angle can be worked in. Trivial events are exaggerated and the yellow press thrives on gossip and scandal-mongering alongside distortions of real news. A good example occurred during the 2008 London mayoral election, when the London *Evening Standard*'s 'misery boards' outside every Tube station screamed 'Islamic militant runs Ken campaign'. This carried the clear implication that Ken Livingstone's campaign for re-election as Mayor of London was being orchestrated by supporters of terrorism. The key absence from the headline was the letter 'a' in front of 'Ken', which would have truthfully revealed that one out of dozens of *unofficial* campaigns was indeed being run by a militant Islamist. The term 'yellow press' is now quite rare – we use 'tabloid' or 'redtop' instead – although 'yellow journalism' is still used, almost always in a derogatory sense.

Yob

A simple piece of backslang that appears to have entered mainstream English in the Victorian era, but was not popularized until the twentieth century. It is really just 'boy' backwards, the implication being that reversing the word shows that something is wrong with the child or youth in question – in this case that the lad is an uncouth ruffian up to no good, and certainly capable of causing aggro (q.v.). Today we tend to say 'ASBO' (from Anti-Social Behaviour Order, a civil order in the UK and Ireland prohibiting certain specified behaviour; breaching an ASBO is a criminal offence) or 'hoodie' (from the hooded tops worn by many yobs) where once we said 'yobbo', but the meaning is the same: a young male engaged in, or likely to be engaged in, anti-social behaviour at best, criminal activities at worst. (Curiously, the adjective 'yobbish' to describe the behaviour is heard far more often than 'yob' or 'yobbo'; 'yobette', for the female equivalent, has never really caught on, and the noun 'yobbery' is also quite uncommon nowadays.) This view of predominantly poor, often poorly educated and sometimes unruly young men is a common thread in British society and one that both the founder of the Scout movement, Robert Baden-Powell, and Rudyard Kipling, as well as several more recent commentators, have railed against. They and others have often pointed out that the demonized yob of peacetime is very often the hero in war (Tommy, q.v.).

Z reservists

Class Z reservists were former servicemen who could be recalled to the forces (of whichever branch) in the event of war, and who attended a two-week training camp every year. A bit like soldiers of the Territorial Army, but without the choice, they could be called up at moments of crisis. In 1956 some Z Reservists baulked at being called up and possibly shipped out to intervene at Suez, and talk of them mutinying caused a certain amount of alarm in military circles.

BIBLIOGRAPHY

Ayto, John (ed.), *Brewer's Dictionary of Phrase and Fable*, seventeenth edition, Chambers Harrap

— and Crofton, Ian (eds), *Brewer's Dictionary of Modern Phrase and Fable*, second edition, Chambers Harrap

Bartleby.com [website – 1898 edition of E. Cobham Brewer's *Dictionary of Phrase and Fable*] <www.bartleby.com/81>

Classic Encylopedia [website – 1911 *Encyclopædia Britannica* online] <www.1911encyclopedia.org>

Dalzell, Tom and Victor, Terry (eds), *The Concise New Partridge Dictionary of Slang and Unconventional English*, Routledge

Dictionary.com [website] <http://dictionary.reference.com/>

Green, Jonathon, *The Penguin Slang Thesaurus*, second edition, Penguin Books

Knowles, Elizabeth (ed.), *Oxford Dictionary of Phrase and Fable*, second edition, Oxford University Press

— (ed.), *Oxford Dictionary of Quotations*, Oxford University Press

Lost for Words [website] <http://etymolog.blogspot.com/>

Phrase Finder, The [website] <http://www.phrases.org.uk/>

Project Gutenberg [website] <www.gutenberg.org>

Simpson, John and Weiner, Edmund (eds), *The Oxford English Dictionary*, second edition (20 volumes), Oxford University Press

UK Television Adverts 1955–85 [website] <www.headington.org.uk>

Wikipedia [website] <www.wikipedia.org>

Word Detective, The [website] <www.word-detective.com>
Wordie [website] <http://wordie.org>
World Wide Words [website] <www.worldwidewords.org>
Yule, Sir Henry, Burnell, A. C. and Crooke, William (eds),
    *Hobson-Jobson: A Glossary of Colloquial Anglo-Indian Words and
    Phrases and of Kindred Items, Etymological, Historical, Geographical
    and Discursive*, Wordsworth Reference

The author and publishers are grateful to the following for
permission to quote copyright material:

John Betjeman: extracts from 'Business Girls' and 'How To
Get On In Society' from *Collected Poems* (John Murray),
copyright © 1955, 1958, 1962, 1964, 1968, 1960, 1979,
1981, 1982, 2001 by John Betjeman, by permission of
John Murray (Publishers), a division of Hachette UK.

Philip Larkin: extract from 'This Be the Verse' from
Collected Poems (Faber and Faber), copyright © 1988, 1989
by the Estate of Philip Larkin, by permission of Faber
and Faber Ltd.